pg

Also by Jessica Faye Carter

DOUBLE OUTSIDERS: HOW WOMEN OF COLOR CAN SUCCEED IN CORPORATE AMERICA

Troubling Her

A BIBLICAL DEFENSE OF WOMEN IN MINISTRY

JESSICA FAYE CARTER

pg

purple girl books

pg

purple girl books

Copyright © 2009 by Jessica Faye Carter
All rights reserved,
including the right of reproduction
in whole or in part in any form.

Unless otherwise noted, all Scripture quotations are from The Holy Bible, English Standard Version® (ESV®), copyright © 2001 by Crossway, a publishing ministry of Good News Publishers. Used by permission. All rights reserved.

Scripture quotations marked NKJV™ are taken from the New King James Version®. Copyright © 1982 by Thomas Nelson, Inc. Used by permission. All rights reserved.

Scripture quotations marked KJV are taken from The Holy Bible, King James Version.

Scripture quotations marked NASB are taken from the New American Standard Bible®, Copyright © 1960, 1962, 1963, 1968, 1971, 1972, 1973, 1975, 1977, 1995 by The Lockman Foundation. Used by permission. (www.Lockman.org)

Cover design by Angi Shearstone
Photo credit: Maria Adelaide Silva

Printed in the United States of America

First Edition: January 2010

ISBN 978-0-578-03454-6

O God, who is like unto thee?
Psalm 71:19, KJV

Table of Contents

Introduction	ix
All the Counsel of God	1
Showing Partiality in Judgment	11
The Image of God	33
Christ and His Followers	43
Understanding First Timothy	59
Human Traditions vs. God's Commands	71
Servants or Rulers?	83
Epilogue: Preparing for the Lord's Return	95
Author's Note	97
Appendix A: Believe on the Lord Jesus Christ	99
Appendix B: Reading and Discussion Questions	101
Index	103

Introduction

Troubling Her is derived from a question that Jesus asked His disciples shortly before His crucifixion. They were all in Bethany at the house of Simon the leper, and as they sat around the table a woman came in, carrying some expensive, fragrant oil. She used it to anoint Jesus.

Jesus' disciples had a strange reaction: they were angry with the woman, viewing her gift as a waste. Instead, they suggested, it should have been sold and the proceeds given to the poor. Jesus saw it differently and praised her gift, noting that she gave it in preparation for His burial. He had so much regard for her actions that He tied the preaching of the gospel to the story of her gift:

> **Matthew 26:6–13**
>
> 6 Now when Jesus was at Bethany in the house of Simon the leper,
>
> 7 a woman came up to him with an alabaster flask of very expensive ointment, and she poured it on his head as he reclined at table.
>
> 8 And when the disciples saw it, they were indignant, saying, "Why this waste?
>
> 9 For this could have been sold for a large sum and given to the poor."
>
> 10 But Jesus, aware of this, said to them, "Why do you trouble the woman? For she has done a beautiful thing to me.
>
> 11 For you always have the poor with you, but you will not always have me.
>
> 12 In pouring this ointment on my body, she has done it to prepare me for burial.
>
> 13 Truly, I say to you, wherever this gospel is proclaimed in the whole world, what she has done will also be told in memory of her."

This woman, who the disciples were troubling, had heard and believed what Christ said concerning His death and resurrection. She brought ointment to anoint His body in preparation for His crucifixion. Her gesture was an intimate one that was full of faith.

The rejection of this woman's gift parallels the way women in ministry are treated today. They have responded to Christ's call and are offering their ministry gifts in faith and obedience to God. Yet they find themselves troubled by some of Christ's male disciples who don't understand the value or purpose of these women's gifts. Christ, however, sees it differently and accepts the women's offerings.

The purpose of this book is to provide women in ministry, or those called to ministry, with biblical support for their efforts. I've heard women say numerous times that they have a distinct sense of being called, or are already in ministry, but feel unsure or not entirely clear about what the Bible teaches on the subject. Even when they are certain of what God is calling them to do, they may lack sufficient knowledge of the Scriptures to defend themselves against the onslaught of naysayers in their denominations, families, and lives.

My study of the Bible on this subject has led me to the conclusion that women are called by God to minister to and lead His people, and have been from ancient times to the present day. Throughout the book, I'll discuss in detail what the Bible teaches about women in ministry by examining relevant verses, narratives, and principles. This includes verses that support, as well as those which seem to disagree with my conclusion. You will see plenty of verses you recognize, along with some you would not expect to be part of the discussion.

Ultimately, you may come to a different conclusion than I did about women in ministry. In such a case, we must agree

Introduction

to disagree. Sincere Christians can come to different conclusions about what the Bible teaches.

But this must also be said: all objections to women in ministry are not sincere. Some of the hindrances women ministers face have nothing to do with what the Bible teaches, and everything to do with those who are interested in preserving their status and power within the Church. There are religious leaders today whose lust for power and position or self-absorption blinds them to the truth about women in ministry, much the same as the Pharisees and scribes rejected the truth of Christ for selfish reasons. Such people are not new to the Body of Christ nor are they likely to go away anytime soon.

If you are a woman called to ministry, as you read this book, remember the boldness of Peter and John at the Beautiful Gate, who, after healing a man were commanded "not to speak at all nor teach in the name of Jesus" (Acts 4:18). This command sounds rather similar to what is said to many women in the Church today. Peter's response to the command was perfect, not only for him but also for women in ministry today:

Acts 4:19–20

19 But Peter and John answered them, "Whether it is right in the sight of God to listen to you rather than to God, you must judge,

20 for we cannot but speak of what we have seen and heard."

When others oppose your calling and efforts, remind them of your requirement to obey God, no matter what they (or anyone else) thinks of your ministry. One day you will answer to God for your actions—the responsibility to obey God is yours.

My prayer for you as you are reading this book, is that God will open your eyes, ears, and heart to the truth of His Word (Pr. 20:12; Eze. 3:10; Luke 24:31; Acts 16:14). That God will grant you the wisdom and the grace to fulfill His calling in Christ Jesus, in accordance with the working of His mighty power, which He worked in Christ when He raised Him from the dead and seated Him in the heavens (Eph. 1:20). I pray that God will encourage your heart and remind you of His faithfulness and mercy, and that you find will find rest in His Word and shelter from the trials and difficulties of ministry.

Let me know how you are doing in ministry and your thoughts about the book. You can reach me via email at: info@troublingher.com.

Jessica Faye Carter
January 10, 2010

CHAPTER ONE
All the Counsel of God

"Where there is no counsel, the people fall; But in the multitude of counselors, there is safety."

PROVERBS 11:14, NKJV

"For I did not shrink from declaring to you the whole counsel of God."

ACTS 20:27

The role of women in ministry continues to be among the most hotly debated issues in Christianity. Questions abound regarding the appropriate function of women in the Church, the world, and at home—and there are a variety of views on the subject.

Denominations vary widely in their practices, from a complete refusal to ordain women to the full ordination of women as pastors and elders. This wide range of interpretation and practice among Christians occurs, in part, because the Bible is ambiguous about this issue. There are examples of women in the Bible chosen by God to lead His people. There are also Bible verses that seem to reject the idea of women as leaders. The ways in which denominations resolve this ambiguity determines their perspective on women in ministry.

So how do we resolve this issue? By examining "all the counsel of God," meaning the wide range of scriptures that relate to women in ministry. We'll study the character and sovereignty of God, the life and ministry of Jesus Christ, creation, women, ministry, marriage, the Church, and we'll look at biblical examples of leaders—men and women.

As we study these issues, it's important to be aware of some of the interpretive errors that have plagued the discussion of women in ministry. In this chapter, we'll examine three different types of errors that occur in biblical interpretation:

- isolating certain Bible verses and reading them apart from their immediate context, and apart from the complete biblical context;
- inconsistent interpretations and application of Bible verses toward different groups; and
- improperly weighing issues—paying too much attention to issues of lesser importance and ignoring issues of great significance.

For the remainder of this chapter, we'll look at these interpretive errors and how they impact the discussion of women in ministry.

No Bible Verse is an Island

People generally treat the Bible as a collection of independent verses, instead of as a cohesive unit. Such views often result in misinterpretations because the verses are being read in isolation and without balance—without reference to other related verses and issues within the Bible. Reading the Bible this way makes it easy to get a lopsided perspective of God's ways.

The issue of isolation crops up repeatedly with women in ministry, because certain verses in the New Testament seem to make clear cut statements about women in leadership. But when you read those verses in light of the rest of the Bible, the issue is not so clear.

The dangers of isolating verses is illustrated in Luke 13, where a religious leader grabs hold of a verse and holds onto it with all his might:

All the Counsel of God

Luke 13:10–17

10 Now [Jesus] was teaching in one of the synagogues on the Sabbath.

11 And behold, there was a woman who had a spirit of infirmity eighteen years, and was bent over and could in no way raise *herself* up.

12 But when Jesus saw her, He called *her* to *Him* and said to her, "Woman, you are loosed from your infirmity."

13 And He laid *His* hands on her, and immediately she was made straight, and glorified God.

14 But the ruler of the synagogue answered with indignation, because Jesus had healed on the Sabbath; and he said to the crowd, "There are six days on which men ought to work; therefore come and be healed on them, and not on the Sabbath day."

15 The Lord then answered him and said, "Hypocrite! Does not each one of you on the Sabbath loose his ox or donkey from the stall, and lead *it* away to water it?

16 "So ought not this woman, being a daughter of Abraham, whom Satan has bound—think of it—for eighteen years, be loosed from this bond on the Sabbath?"

17 And when He said these things, all His adversaries were put to shame; and all the multitude rejoiced for all the glorious things that were done by Him.

The synagogue ruler's response revealed his myopic view of Scripture. He was convinced that the proper response to the situation was to invoke the Sabbath laws (Exod. 23:12; Deut. 5:13–14). From his perspective, the verse on the Sabbath was obvious in its meaning and it clearly represented God's will on the matter. He knew that he had made his decision based on Scripture.

So how did this religious leader totally miss the boat? By focusing on the Sabbath law to the exclusion of the rest of God's Word. He allowed his own perspective to blind him to alternate ways of understanding the situation. To him, it looked like disobedience to God's laws concerning the Sabbath, so he approached it from that standpoint.

Unfortunately for him, his decision-making process ignored some really important information—the miraculous healing, for instance. In the Jewish Scriptures (what Christians refer to as the Old Testament), healings and other miracles were usually done through a prophet of God (2 Kgs. 4:27–35; 5:9–15). So why didn't the ruler consider, that at the very least, a prophet of God was in Israel? Because he was focused *only* on the Sabbath laws, not the miracle. He focused on what God had said, while ignoring what God was *doing*. The ruler was so off-base that he ended up trying to rebuke Jesus—the very God who spoke the Sabbath laws into existence.

By making the entire situation about the Sabbath the ruler missed another important issue: God's covenant with Abraham. Jesus was careful to remind the ruler that the woman was a daughter of Abraham and that she had been ill for many years. Think about it: the ruler suggested that the woman come back another day to be healed—as if she could just come back any day and be made well. The woman had been sick for 18 years! Obviously she couldn't come on just any day and be healed.

This demonstrated the ruler's lack of attention to God's covenant with Abraham. This man evidently did not consider the woman's healing as a blessing from their covenant-keeping God. Why? Because for the synagogue leader, the entire situation was governed by the Sabbath laws, and the command was clear. So as far as he could tell, he was right.

Except he was wrong.

Sure, he quoted the verse correctly, but he did not understand what it meant in relation to the rest of the Scriptures. He couldn't make sense of the Sabbath, Jesus, the miracle and the woman, so he relied on one set of verses. Even worse, he thought he had a zeal for God, but he was actually fighting against God's Son.

This should come as no surprise. Then, as now, religious leaders quote from the Bible about what is proper concerning women. They latch onto specific verses that seem obvious to them and refuse to let go, even when it becomes obvious that the verse isn't giving them a full picture of what God is doing with respect to women.

The outcome of this narrative is also illuminating: God miraculously healed a woman in a synagogue on the Sabbath. God was glorified. The people rejoiced. Only the synagogue ruler and those with him were angry and ashamed. Not just because Christ pointed out their hypocrisy, but because they realized—in front of everyone—that they really didn't understand the Sabbath laws. God was working through this man on the Sabbath to heal a woman, and they were not included!

This is very similar to what is happening in Christian circles where women in ministry are opposed. God is using women all over the world to preach the gospel and to minister to His Church. The gifts and callings of these women are evident. But in the face of all of this evidence, their leaders continue holding on to a verse or two that they really don't understand. And they do this, despite having a clear example of their behavior set forth in Scripture.

You'll see this scriptural isolation surface as we examine verses related to women in ministry that have not been understood in light of the rest of the Bible, including 1 Timothy 2, 1 Corinthians 14, Ephesians 5 and others.

Inconsistent Application of Scripture

Another interpretive error that impacts women in ministry is the inconsistent application of the Scriptures. This occurs when the same verses are applied inconsistently to different subjects or situations.

Revisiting the Luke 13 narrative above, we see that not only did the religious leaders misunderstand the Sabbath laws, but they also applied those laws inconsistently—in a way that benefitted animals, but not a sick woman:

> Luke 13:15–16
>
> **15 Then the Lord answered him, "You hypocrites! Does not each of you on the Sabbath untie his ox or his donkey from the manger and lead it away to water it?**
>
> **16 And ought not this woman, a daughter of Abraham whom Satan bound for eighteen years, be loosed from this bond on the Sabbath day?**

As Jesus observed, releasing an ox or donkey on the Sabbath had never been a problem in the community. The ruler's problem was that Jesus had healed a *woman*. But the leader was blind to his own conduct, not making the connection between how he treated animals on the Sabbath and the healing of the woman. That is, until Jesus pointed it out.

What makes the ruler's error worse is that women are created in the image of God, and animals are not (Gen. 1:26–27; 2:18–23). So the religious leaders, who were supposed to be honoring God, were more concerned about the animals than with the woman's well-being. No wonder they were ashamed when Jesus rebuked them.

Note that Christ didn't respond to the ruler's Sabbath argument with more Scripture. The problem wasn't that the ruler didn't know the Word—it was that he applied it inconsistently. This same mindset prevents many Christians today from properly applying the Bible consistently to the issue of women in ministry.

These types of inconsistent interpretations have long obscured important teachings about women prophets (e.g.,

Miriam, Deborah, and Huldah), the important revelation given to Martha, and how Paul's recommendation of Phoebe must change our understanding of the role of women in church leadership. We'll look more into these verses later on.

Weighing Scripture

In Matthew 23, Jesus severely criticized the scribes and Pharisees for their behavior in religious matters. One of the complaints He lodged against them related to their improper emphasis on different parts of Scripture. They emphasized issues of lesser importance, while virtually ignoring issues of great importance to God:

> **Matthew 23:23–24**
>
> 23 "Woe to you, scribes and Pharisees, hypocrites! For you tithe mint and dill and cumin, and have neglected the weightier matters of the law: justice and mercy and faithfulness. These you ought to have done, without neglecting the others.
>
> 24 You blind guides, straining out a gnat and swallowing a camel!

These religious leaders were so attentive to God's commands about tithing that they paid tithes of herbs grown in their gardens. Think about how small 10% of a bunch of herbs would have been. But those same leaders, who were so attentive to small amounts of plants, neglected justice, mercy, and faith—things of greater importance to God. It's important to note that Jesus was not presenting them with an either/or scenario. He expected them to tithe and to show forth justice, mercy, and faith. So why were they focusing on one and neglecting the others?

The context of Jesus' remarks provides a clue. Much of the substance of Christ's rebuke of the religious leaders focused on their love of appearances—the things visible to others—while they ignored invisible, eternal matters important to God. This helps us to understand at least part of why they chose to focus on the tithe, as opposed to mercy: because it was something others could see (tithes were presented publicly).

There is more to Christ's criticism of the leaders. In verse 24, He referred to their practice of straining gnats out of their drinks to avoid being unclean, a behavior designed to comply with Leviticus 11:20-23. But, as Christ notes, they then swallowed a camel, which is also unclean (Lev. 11:4).

By designating both the gnat and camel as unclean under the Law, God signified His concern for the tiniest and greatest matters with His people. But the contrast between the gnat and camel also points to the relative importance of issues before God.

The religious leaders were overly concerned with smaller issues (gnats) while paying little attention to major issues (camels). They were scrupulous about the relatively minor aspects of God's Law—particularly the things that gained them visibility—but neglected the things that mattered most to God.

In one sense, those who oppose women in ministry are similarly focused on outward appearances. Their primary concern is the gender of those in Church leadership roles, a view they insist is consistent with Scripture. But as we see from Matthew 23 (and Luke 13 above), holding a view that seems consistent with Scripture doesn't prevent you from being seriously wrong.

Gender is not mentioned in Scripture as God's primary focus in choosing leaders. People are concerned with visible attributes, such as height, weight, gender, skin color, and good looks. But God looks at the heart:

1 Samuel 16:7

But the LORD said to Samuel, "Do not look on his appearance or on the height of his stature, because I have rejected him. For the LORD sees not as man sees: man looks on the outward appearance, but the LORD looks on the heart."

There is a difference in how human beings perceive things and how God sees things. People rely on their eyesight, which is limited, and end up focusing on visible attributes when choosing leaders. Did you notice that God had to warn even the prophet Samuel against regarding good looks or height? It is a human tendency to regard such things, because human vision only reaches so far.

But God's sight is unlimited, reaching well beyond human vision, and penetrating into the hearts of humanity. When God selects leaders, He does so based on the things that He sees—things invisible to the human eye, like the heart. In fact, the value that God places on the human heart is so high that the Book of Proverbs compares it to the value human beings put on silver and gold (Prov. 17:3).

As we study women in ministry, we'll look at some of the leaders chosen by God (male and female) in order to understand more about the character of God and how it impacts the issue of women in ministry.

* * *

Isolating, inconsistently applying, and improperly weighing Scripture can result in the misinterpretation of biblical doctrines related to women in ministry.

To avoid these kinds of interpretive errors as we study, we will examine the Bible in its fullness—not just in terms of picking and choosing Bible verses that appear to support our arguments, but also looking at a wide range of Scriptures. The Bible speaks repeatedly about the wisdom of relying on a wide array of sources when rendering any sort of judgment or interpretation of a matter (Deut. 17:6; 19:15; Matt. 18:15–16; 2 Cor. 13:1; 1 Tim. 5:19). We will also be careful to apply the Scriptures consistently to different groups, as well as give the various biblical teachings their proper weight before God.

The next chapter will examine how human bias impacts the interpretation of Scriptures related to women in ministry. We'll spot some of the errors and learn more about what the Bible teaches about the character of God.

CHAPTER TWO
Showing Partiality in Judgment

"My brethren, do not hold the faith of our Lord Jesus Christ, the Lord of glory, with partiality."

JAMES 2:1, NKJV

"For there is no partiality with God."

ROMANS 2:11

We all like to think that our interpretations of the Bible are pure, free from error, and without bias. But we should realize that, as human beings, our interpretations are filtered through our lives, cultural backgrounds, and biases. This doesn't necessarily make our interpretations wrong, but it does underscore the need for testing biblical teachings, even when they seem to come directly from the Word.

When it comes to the subject of women generally or in ministry, biblical interpretations are often shaded by people's own feelings and perceptions about women, along with their cultural understandings of gender roles. In other words, people interpret the Bible with partiality. In this chapter, we will take a look at partiality in biblical interpretation and examine how it impacts biblical teachings on women in ministry.

What is Partiality?

Partiality is prejudice for or against a thing, person, or group when compared with another—usually in an unfair way. It impacts everyone in the Body of Christ, not just women.

In his letter, the Apostle James confronted partiality in the Church head-on and condemned it:

James 2:1–9

1 My brothers, show no partiality as you hold the faith in our Lord Jesus Christ, the Lord of glory.

2 For if a man wearing a gold ring and fine clothing comes into your assembly, and a poor man in shabby clothing also comes in,

3 and if you pay attention to the one who wears the fine clothing and say, "You sit here in a good place," while you say to the poor man, "You stand over there," or, "Sit down at my feet,"

4 have you not then made distinctions among yourselves and become judges with evil thoughts?

5 Listen, my beloved brothers, has not God chosen those who are poor in the world to be rich in faith and heirs of the kingdom, which he has promised to those who love him?

6 But you have dishonored the poor man. Are not the rich the ones who oppress you, and the ones who drag you into court?

7 Are they not the ones who blaspheme the honorable name by which you were called?

8 If you really fulfill the royal law according to the Scripture, "You shall love your neighbor as yourself," you are doing well.

9 But if you show partiality, you are committing sin and are convicted by the law as transgressors.

The situation James used in his letter is one commonly encountered in society: the rich are treated well, while the poor are mistreated and despised. While we expect to see such treatment in the world, it is not the appropriate standard of conduct for churches.

Humanity tends to judge others based on external appearances, and favors those who are perceived to have an advantage, because of wealth, beauty, fame, or the like. The Apostle James condemns such partiality as sin—an offense to God.

Showing Partiality in Judgment

James viewed partiality as inconsistent with faith in Jesus Christ for several reasons. First, the economic status of a person has no bearing on their relationship with God—in fact, God often chooses the poor as heirs to His Kingdom (v. 5).

The comparison of rich and poor people also brings to mind a proverb:

> **Proverbs 22:2**
>
> **The rich and the poor meet together; the LORD is the maker of them all.**

To God, the rich and the poor are both in the same category: God's creation (Prov. 22:2). So another reason we are not to show partiality is out of respect for God.

We are also not to be partial because God shows no partiality in his dealings with humanity (Deut. 10:17; 2 Chr. 19:7; Rom. 2:11). As Christians, we are to be imitators of God (Eph. 5:1). This includes treating everyone with respect, without regard to their external characteristics.

The issue of partiality is important because it has significantly impacted the study of women in the Bible, including women in ministry. The partiality James described involved selective attention to people of different economic statuses, but this principle can also apply to biblical interpretation. In this chapter, we will examine the selective interpretation of the Bible as it relates to women in ministry, because much of the Bible has been selectively taught, interpreted, and applied in ways that diminish women.

Selective Interpretation of the Bible

In biblical teaching about women, including women in ministry, partiality in interpretation and selective use of the Scriptures is widespread. Verses with requirements for women are overemphasized, while those with requirements for men are referenced much less often.

Biblical narratives with women in leadership or ministry positions are often ignored or dismissed as insignificant, while ministry requirements are assumed to not include women. This selective emphasis has resulted in considerable error in Church doctrine concerning women in leadership.

Below are some examples of selective interpretation impacting women in ministry.

Wives and Husbands

When it comes to women and wives, selective interpretation is the norm. Probably the most prominent example of partiality is found in Ephesians 5. Christian teaching on marriage tends to emphasize Ephesians 5:22, while ignoring the previous verse—Ephesians 5:21:

> **Ephesians 5:21–22**
> **21 submitting to one another out of reverence for Christ.**
> **22 Wives, submit to your own husbands, as to the Lord.**

Submission is not limited to wives in the Body of Christ. It is meant to characterize everyone's behavior in the family. But because of partiality, Christians have focused on wives being submissive and have ignored the command that everyone be submissive. Many Christians are unaware that verse 21 even exists.

Interpretations of 1 Peter 3 often include a similar interpretive bias:

> **1 Peter 3:5–6**
> **5 For this is how the holy women who hoped in God used to adorn themselves, by submitting to their own husbands,**

Showing Partiality in Judgment

> **6** as Sarah obeyed Abraham, calling him lord. And you are her children, if you do good and do not fear anything that is frightening.

Many teachers focus on Sarah's obedience to Abraham, and conveniently forget to read the original story in Genesis—the one where God told Abraham to obey His wife:[1]

> **Genesis 21:12**
>
> But God said to Abraham, "Be not displeased because of the boy and because of your slave woman. Whatever Sarah says to you, do as she tells you, for through Isaac shall your offspring be named.

"Do as Sarah tells you" was God's command to Abraham. How many times have you heard that taught about Sarah and Abraham's relationship? It plainly indicates that husbands also submit to their wives.

If you read the conclusion of Peter's letter, in which the story of Sarah and Abraham is mentioned, he tells the congregation they are *all* to be humble toward each another, for God resists the proud, but gives grace to the humble (1 Pe. 5:5). Remember that mutuality is a key principle of God's doctrine—godly relationships are not one-sided.

Still, the majority of Christian teachings have required that the wife show humility and be submissive and have neglected to teach that the husband is also to do those same things (Eph. 5:21, 25, 28; 1 Pet. 3:8; 5:5). As these verses note, *everyone* in the Body of Christ is to show these characteristics, not just women and wives. Remember, Christ is everyone's example of submissiveness and humility—and He is male.
God's commands are not one-sided; they are always mutual and balanced. There are commands for wives and husbands, parents and children, and those enslaved and masters (Eph. 5:21-23; 6:1-9; 1 Cor. 7:4). When you hear a discussion that

overemphasizes the biblical responsibilities of only one group, such as women, it's selective teaching.

Women and Wives

There is also confusion in many churches related to women and wives in biblical doctrine, as if doctrines related to wives apply to women generally. Part of the reason this occurs is because the Greek words for wife and woman are the same; the words for husband and male are also the same. As a result, it is necessary to look for clues in the rest of the narrative to determine whether the issues discussed relate to wives or women generally. Sometimes it's difficult to be sure.

When seeking to understand the role of women in ministry, it doesn't make sense to focus on Scriptures related to wives—because many women in ministry are single and such verses are not relevant to their lives and ministries. In other words, any doctrine that is meant to apply to women will not be solely focused on wives, or else it won't include about half the population of women!

Here's an example of a teaching that has been wrongly applied to all women, when it is more likely directed to certain women in the congregation:

> **1 Corinthians 14:34–35**
>
> **34 Let your women keep silent in the churches, for they are not permitted to speak; but** *they are* **to be submissive, as the law also says.**
>
> **35 And if they want to learn something, let them ask their own husbands at home; for it is shameful for women to speak in church.**

Some Christians believe that these verses command women to keep silent in church, but it's more likely that Paul was referring to certain women only. How do we know this?

First, he mentioned that the women should direct their questions to their husbands—women he was referring to were married. We know from the rest of Paul's letter to the Corinthians, all of the women in the congregation were not married (1 Cor. 7:8). Taken literally, this command couldn't have applied to the single women.

Further, Paul implied that the husbands of the women knew enough doctrine to answer (or get answers to) the women's questions. But this statement wasn't even true of all of the married women in the congregation—some of them had husbands who weren't believers (1 Cor. 7:12-16). Paul wasn't advising Christian women to ask their unsaved husbands for clarification on the Word!

If we read 1 Corinthians 14:34-35 in the context of the rest of 1 Corinthians we find even more to think about. As an example, in 1 Corinthians 11:5, Paul writes that women praying or prophesying should cover their heads. But in order to pray or prophesy, the woman would have to speak, right? So within 1 Corinthians, Paul seems to prohibit women from speaking, but then requires them to wear certain attire when they do speak. So women obviously spoke in church.

This gives you a sense of how difficult it is to interpret Paul's writings, because we only have his responses and don't have access to the original questions asked of him. But with respect to 1 Cor. 14:34-35, we have enough information from the rest of 1 Corinthians to conclude that Paul was referring to specific women with his command—not all women. Women most certainly can and should speak in church.

Christ, the Hebrew Man

The identity of Christ is another major example of selective biblical interpretation related to women in ministry. You may have heard the argument that Christ's incarnation as a man is proof that only men are qualified to hold leadership roles in the Church. This is a selective argument because it focuses on Christ's maleness and ignores the fact that Christ was also Hebrew.

The Scriptures prophesied that Christ was to be a Hebrew male—the seed of Abraham and the Son of David (Gen. 5:15; Matt. 1:1; Gal. 3:16). We must consider both of these aspects of Christ's earthly identity when working to understand the implications of Christ's identity for women in ministry and Church leadership, instead of only focusing on Christ's maleness.

If we apply the arguments typically used to disqualify women from ministry, we will find that they also disqualify Gentiles from ministry. Christ came as a Hebrew, and all of the 12 apostles were Hebrew (Acts 2:7). In the Old Testament, the entire priesthood was Hebrew (Exod. 28:1; Lev. 21:1). Does anyone interpret this to mean that only Hebrews can lead in the Church?

No.

So if the fact that Christ, the apostles, the prophets and all the Old Testament priests were Hebrew doesn't exclude Gentiles from Church leadership, then the fact that Christ, the apostles and the Old Testament priests were male does not exclude women from Church leadership, either.

The reality is that Christ existed as the Word of God from all eternity (John 1:1). His taking on of human flesh was part of God's plan to save His people (Matt. 1:21; 1 Tim. 3:16). Nothing in the New Testament indicates that the advent of Christ was a statement by God as to the superiority of any ethnic group or gender.

Ignoring Women Ministers in the Bible

The other way that selective biblical interpretation impacts women in ministry is by ignoring or minimizing the roles of women in leadership, even though God has documented their callings and work in the Bible. By examining some of these women and their ministries, we get a better understanding of how God calls and equips women to fulfill His will.

Miriam

Miriam's story is a perfect example of selective biblical interpretation. Most of today's biblical teaching on Miriam is limited to Miriam as the sister of Moses (Num. 26:59), who guarded him when he was a baby (Exod. 2:4), led the women in dance after crossing the Red Sea (Exod. 15:20–21), and who spoke against Moses' marriage to an Ethiopian woman (Num. 12:1–9).

What most current teaching manages to ignore is the rest (and more important part) of the Bible's description of Miriam: a woman called by God to be a prophet (Exod. 15:20–21), one of the leaders of Israel (Mic. 6:4), and one through whom God spoke (Num. 12:2).

Miriam's status as a prophet means that she heard directly from God and spoke on behalf of God. The Hebrew words for male and female prophets come from the root *naba*, which means "to speak or prophesy by a divine power." Miriam did not promote herself to become a prophet, nor was she a prophet because she was Moses' sister. She was directly chosen by God (Num. 12:6). She was also mentioned along with Moses and Aaron as those sent by God to lead Israel out of Egypt (Mic. 6:4).[2] Miriam was one of the leaders of Israel.

Deborah

Deborah's ministry has been severely downplayed in Christian circles. She was a prophet and judge of Israel who was raised up by God in response to the cries of the Israelites, as all the Judges were (Judg. 2:11-16; 4:3–4).

Deborah is described as sitting, which in the Hebrew (*shaphat*) signifies that she was presiding or ruling over Israel. Deborah was a woman with authority. She heard from God, decided disputes between the people, commanded Barak (a man) and delivered the word of the Lord (Judg. 4:6–10). She even had a specific place (a palm tree) where people could come to her to learn God's judgments (Judg. 4:5).

Deborah's actions are the same types of activities that Moses engaged in (Exod. 18:13-16), as well as Samuel (1 Sam. 17:15-17), both very prominent Old Testament prophets. All of these verses use the same Hebrew verb to describe the prophet's judging actions. So how is it that some are minimizing Deborah's role as if she didn't really do very much? Because of selective interpretation.

Some teachings suggest that Judges was a period of falling away and returning and should not be considered a norm for leadership. Others suggest that men weren't doing their part as leaders, which is why God chose a woman. But God does not have to settle for leaders from what's available—God *raised up* the judges (Judg. 2:16-19)! The suggestion that God couldn't find anyone better than Deborah is simply untrue. God does not look for leaders, God makes them.

Leaders exist only because God promotes them into positions of power (Rom. 13:1), and the same God that raised up Moses and Samuel also raised up Deborah. There is nothing in the Bible to suggest that God's selection of Deborah was anything other than God's sovereign choice.

Some have suggested that Barak, and not Deborah, was the true leader of Israel, because he is mentioned by name in the Hebrews 11 list of heroes of the faith. But Deborah (and the other women prophets) are also mentioned in Hebrews 11—in the group called "prophets" in Hebrews 11:32.

One final note concerning Deborah—she was married. There is no indication that her authoritative ministry was incompatible with marriage and family. The same is also true for the prophet Huldah, also married, who we'll discuss next.

Huldah

Huldah was a woman prophet of God, whose ministry coincided with other well-known prophets like Jeremiah and Zephaniah. She was sought out by the High Priest and scribes after the High Priest found the book of the Law in the House of the Lord. When the scribe read the book to King Josiah, he tore his clothes and commanded the High Priest, scribes, one of his servants, and a few others to inquire of the Lord. The King didn't tell them *who* to go see, he just told them to get God's thoughts. The High Priest and scribes went to Huldah to get the Word of the Lord:

> **2 Kings 22:14-16**
>
> **14 So Hilkiah the priest, and Ahikam, and Achbor, and Shaphan, and Asaiah went to Huldah the prophetess, the wife of Shallum the son of Tikvah, son of Harhas, keeper of the wardrobe (now she lived in Jerusalem in the Second Quarter), and they talked with her.**
>
> **15 And she said to them, "Thus says the LORD, the God of Israel: 'Tell the man who sent you to me,**
>
> **16 Thus says the LORD, Behold, I will bring disaster upon this place and upon its inhabitants, all the words of the book that the king of Judah has read...**

So God spoke to the men (including the High Priest) through Huldah, and gave them a message for King Josiah. The religious leaders trusted Huldah as a prophet of God to deliver the Word of the Lord, and she did. On the basis of what she told the men, King Josiah enacted reforms that brought Israel back to observing the Mosaic Law in a way which had not been done since the days of the prophet Samuel (2 Chr. 35:18).

Huldah's place of residence provides us with another clue about her role in Israel. In Hebrew, the phrase Second Quarter (*mishneh*) means to copy and comes from the root *shanah*, which means to repeat. Most likely the place was similar to a college, where the Law was taught by oral repetition and passed down, or perhaps where scribes copied the Law. So it makes sense that the High Priest and scribes would have gone to Huldah to ask about the Law. She was a teacher of it.

Some have questioned why Huldah delivered the Word of the Lord instead of Jeremiah or Zephaniah. This is a silly question. It is the word of the *Lord*, not the word of Jeremiah or Zephaniah. God can use whatever vessel He chooses. They are all His servants.

The bottom line is this: in the Old Testament, God called women to lead His people, and to proclaim His Word as prophets, judges, rulers, and teachers. Today, we have a better covenant with God, established with better promises (Heb. 8:6), so it is not surprising that God continues to use women in leadership roles among His people.

Priscilla

In the New Testament, Priscilla is described as a teacher (Acts 18:26), fellow laborer of Paul, and a pastor:

> **Romans 16:3–5**
>
> **3 Greet Prisca and Aquila, my fellow workers in Christ Jesus,**
>
> **4 who risked their necks for my life, to whom not only I give thanks but all the churches of the Gentiles give thanks as well.**
>
> **5 Greet also the church in their house. Greet my beloved Epaenetus, who was the first convert to Christ in Asia.**

Priscilla ministered together with her husband Aquila; they are generally mentioned together. Paul describes the church as being in their house, not just his house. Some have suggested that Priscilla was only allowed to teach and minister because she was working with her husband, but there is no evidence of this in the Bible. It seems more likely that, as with the women who ministered in the Old Testament, Priscilla was called by God to minister, and she also happened to be married.

The ministries of these women in the Old and New Testaments provide clear evidence that God chooses women to lead His people. The issue is not one of gender, but of calling. (If you're wondering what to make of the Apostle Paul's instruction to Timothy about women teachers, I discuss it in chapter 5.)

Ministry Qualifications

The mention of Phoebe, a deacon at the church of Cenchrea, in Paul's epistle (letter) to the church at Rome is very important. This is because the criteria for deacons discussed in 1 Timothy seems to only include men:

> **1 Timothy 3:8–13**
>
> **8 Deacons likewise must be dignified, not double-tongued, not addicted to much wine, not greedy for dishonest gain.**
>
> **9 They must hold the mystery of the faith with a clear conscience.**
>
> **10 And let them also be tested first; then let them serve as deacons if they prove themselves blameless.**
>
> **11 Their wives likewise must be dignified, not slanderers, but sober-minded, faithful in all things.**
>
> **12 Let deacons each be the husband of one wife, managing their children and their own households well.**
>
> **13 For those who serve well as deacons gain a good standing for themselves and also great confidence in the faith that is in Christ Jesus.**

Because of verse 12, some Christians today argue that the requirement that a deacon be "the husband of one wife" necessitates that deacons be male. But in Romans 16, Paul has specifically described Phoebe as a deacon, so there were evidently male and female deacons. The Greek word Paul uses to describe Phoebe is *diakonos*, which means (and can be translated) servant and is the origin of the English word deacon. Paul also calls Phoebe a "sister," which indicates beyond any doubt that Paul is describing a woman.

So how do we reconcile Phoebe, a woman deacon, and the requirement that a deacon be the "husband of one wife"? One possibility is that Paul, in saying "one wife," was addressing polygamy, a practice which continues to exist in certain parts of the world today. But one thing is certain: since Paul has acknowledged Phoebe as a deacon, and recommends that the church receive her, he cannot be understood as rejecting the idea of women deacons. Keep in mind that Paul sent not only his own regards, but also Timothy's (Rom. 16:21) through Phoebe, who seems to have delivered the letter to the congregation (Rom. 16:1).

Here's another possibility: Paul may have made reference to male deacons and also meant to include women deacons, but didn't say so explicitly. Jesus, during His ministry, showed that even when it seems like God is talking about men, there are instances in which God intends to include women:

Mark 10:10–12

10 And in the house the disciples asked him again about this matter.

11 And he said to them, "Whoever divorces his wife and marries another commits adultery against her,

12 and if she divorces her husband and marries another, she commits adultery."

Here, Jesus specifically mentions that a woman can divorce her husband and marry someone else. But if you read the Old Testament laws, it does not appear that women even had the right to divorce their husbands, because the women weren't specifically mentioned as having such a right:

> **Deuteronomy 24:1**
>
> "When a man takes a wife and marries her, if then she finds no favor in his eyes because he has found some indecency in her, and he writes her a certificate of divorce and puts it in her hand and sends her out of his house, and she departs out of his house..."

Reading this verse literally would mean that only men had the right to divorce their wives. But when Christ references that verse, He is clearly including women as having the right to divorce their husbands, just as men could divorce their wives:

> **Mark 10:11–12**
>
> 11 And he said to them, "Whoever divorces his wife and marries another commits adultery against her,
>
> 12 and if she divorces her husband and marries another, she commits adultery."

Now since Christ stated clearly that He did not come to abolish the Law (Matt. 5:17), we know that He is not changing the Old Testament command. Rather, he is *clarifying* it so that we understand that while it appeared to apply only to men, it also applied to women.

While this teaching may seem new to you, it is important to realize that Christians already interpret certain Bible verses this way:

> **Luke 14:26**
>
> "If anyone comes to me and does not hate his own father and mother and wife and children and brothers and sisters, yes, and even his own life, he cannot be my disciple.

This verse describes what a disciple of Christ must be prepared to sacrifice. It mentions a person leaving everything he knows to follow Christ, including his wife. At first glance, this would seem to imply that the disciple must be a man.

The Gospels has several examples of people besides the disciples (including women) who also followed Christ (Luke 8:1–3). These women were so involved with Christ's ministry that they were part of the group of disciples who saw Christ ascend into heaven, and who waited for and were baptized in the Holy Spirit (Acts 1:12–15; 2:1–4). Christians have generally understood the requirements of discipleship as applying to everyone—men and women.

The Greek translation is consistent with this interpretation. In the Greek, the word that we translate "anyone" is *tis*, meaning someone or anyone. It is not a specifically male or female term. Had God intended for discipleship to only apply to men, the word used would have specifically referred to males.

The use of this pronoun (*tis*) is not limited to disciples, it's also used in 1 Timothy when describing the qualifications for a bishop:

1 Timothy 3:1–2

1 The saying is trustworthy: If anyone aspires to the office of overseer, he desires a noble task.

2 Therefore an overseer must be above reproach, the husband of one wife, sober-minded, self-controlled, respectable, hospitable, able to teach...

Here we see a combination of the above examples. The "anyone" mentioned in verse 1 refers to any person who aspires, whether male or female. Some translations read "if any man" instead of "any person," but in Greek the term includes men and women.

Some have used the phrase "husband of one wife" to mean that women can't be bishops. But what did we just learn about this "husband of one wife" language when it was used for deacons? We learned that Paul's use of that phrase did not prevent him from acknowledging and working with women deacons. Just as with deacons, Paul's use of this "one wife" phrase should not be interpreted as a prohibition against women bishops, any more than the same phrase prohibited women deacons.

Ultimately, when we read Bible verses that seem to apply only to men with spouses, we now know that those verses can also apply to women. But because many biblical teachers have selectively studied and taught these issues, many people continue to have a misunderstanding about women in ministry.

Selective Application of the Bible

The third area where partiality surfaces in the discussion of women in ministry is in the selective application of the Bible—where different biblical standards are used for men and women. An example of this partiality occurs in John 8, where the scribes and Pharisees brought a woman to Jesus who was caught in adultery:

> **John 8:3–6**
>
> **3 The scribes and the Pharisees brought a woman who had been caught in adultery, and placing her in the midst**
>
> **4 they said to him, "Teacher, this woman has been caught in the act of adultery.**
>
> **5 Now in the Law Moses commanded us to stone such women. So what do you say?"**
>
> **6 This they said to test him, that they might have some charge to bring against him. Jesus bent down and wrote with his finger on the ground.**

By bringing only the woman caught in adultery to Jesus, the religious leaders were showing partiality or bias in their judgment. Was the woman committing adultery by herself? Of course not. So why didn't the religious leaders bring the man she was with? Partiality. Even the Old Testament verse they cited to Jesus about adultery condemns both people caught in the act:

> **Leviticus 20:10**
> **If a man commits adultery with the wife of his neighbor, both the adulterer and the adulteress shall surely be put to death.**

Had the scribes and Pharisees been truly zealous for God's Law, they would have followed it completely and brought both the man and the woman to the Lord. But they only brought the woman. They were looking to apply God's laws with bias—to the woman, but not to the man. Not surprisingly, the Lord ignored them and refused to take part in their little sham proceeding.

When the religious leaders pressed Jesus, He reminded them of their own inability to keep the Law (John 8:6–9; 1 John 3:4). Of course, Jesus didn't approve of her sin and told her to stop the behavior, so it seems that she was guilty (John 8:10–11). But the Lord would not condemn her, because God refuses to show partiality in judgment—and He will not participate with us when we do.

While this narrative does not specifically mention women in ministry, it provides an illustration of how religious leaders interpret the Scriptures in ways that are biased against women. For women in ministry, the selective application of the Bible against women impacts not only their involvement in Christianity, but also their ministry efforts.

Often this selective application is practical in nature. In some denominations there is a significant emphasis on women's attire: hair, makeup, jewelry, pants or skirts—with no similar emphasis on men's attire. Women ministers often find themselves managing objections and issues related to their appearance that male ministers do not even have to consider. These and similar types of issues take women's time and attention away from ministry.

God, the Impartial Judge

As noted earlier in this chapter, the main reason that partiality is unacceptable to God is because it conflicts with God's character. God is an impartial, incorruptible judge who rewards and punishes each person according to his or her work:

> 2 Chronicles 19:7
>
> "Now then, let the fear of the LORD be upon you. Be careful what you do, for there is no injustice with the LORD our God, or partiality or taking bribes."

> 1 Peter 1:17
>
> "And if you call on him as Father who judges impartially according to each one's deeds, conduct yourselves with fear throughout the time of your exile,

God is not influenced by wealth, celebrity, attractiveness, race, gender or any other external characteristic, because He is the maker of all (Neh. 9:6; Prov. 22:2; Acts 17:24).

We see further evidence of God's impartiality in God's insistence that only one law be used to govern Israel, including strangers who had joined themselves to the community. God would not allow multiple laws to govern different groups of people under His authority. All were bound to follow one law:

> **Exodus 12:49**
>
> **There shall be one law for the native and for the stranger who sojourns among you."**

> **Leviticus 24:22**
>
> **You shall have the same rule for the sojourner and for the native, for I am the LORD your God."**

While these requirements focus on "one law," there is also an implicit requirement that the "one law" be applied consistently. God would hardly require that the community be governed by one law and then allow that law to be applied with partiality to different groups. The administration of the law must also be without bias.

Proverbs makes reference to this issue, but in a different way:

> **Proverbs 20:10**
>
> **Unequal weights and unequal measures are both alike an abomination to the LORD.**

> **Proverbs 20:23**
>
> **Unequal weights are an abomination to the LORD, and false scales are not good.**

These proverbs originally referenced merchants who weighed things in a fraudulent manner so that they would benefit. The merchants carried multiple weights with them—the heavier weights for use in sales (so they would make more money) and the lighter ones for use in purchases (so they would pay out less money). The essence of their dishonesty was that it was self-serving.

This was a practice that God viewed (and still views) as an abomination, because God is just, and commands that a consistent weight be used for all transactions. This sentiment was echoed elsewhere in the Law and the Prophets (Lev. 19:36; Deut. 25:13; Micah 6:11).

If God finds dishonest scales and weights to be abominable when they deal with regular goods and services, how much more abominable does God find dishonest, self-serving biblical interpretations? Especially when the interpretations suggest that God is partial to a particular type of person for ministry.

When it comes to women in ministry, some Christians argue that because God created everyone, He is under no obligation to treat or judge them equally. They insist that God does not treat men and women equally when it comes to ministry. God is certainly sovereign, but God absolutely rejects the notion that He is in any way partial or unjust:

Ezekiel 18:29

Yet the house of Israel says, 'The way of the Lord is not just.' O house of Israel, are my ways not just? Is it not your ways that are not just?

Here, when God was accused of being unjust, God's response indicated that it was actually His accusers who were unjust. In like manner, those who suggest that God prefers men to women in ministry are really only showing their own bias— because God is not biased and doesn't select leaders that way (1 Sam. 16:7).

NOTES

1. The only biblical record of Sarah calling Abraham Lord occurs when she is laughing at the idea of having a child (Gen. 18:12).

2. Miriam's importance to the Israelite community is underscored by the fact that the camp didn't travel until she was received back into the community, despite her punishment (Num. 12:15).

CHAPTER THREE
The Image of God

"[Jesus] answered and said to them, 'Have you not read that He who made them at the beginning 'made them male and female?'"

MATTHEW 19:4

One major concept undergirding the arguments against women in ministry is the idea that women do not bear the image of God. Or that women are less of the image of God than men because of the order of creation or as a result of the fall.

These ideas are completely false.

In this chapter, we will examine what it means to be in the image of God, the role of creation in determining this image, the impact of the fall upon that image, and the implications of all these things upon women in ministry.

Woman Was Created in the Image of God

The creation of humanity was described in the first creation account of Genesis:

> **Genesis 1:26–28**
>
> 26 Then God said, "Let us make man in our image, after our likeness. And let them have dominion over the fish of the sea and over the birds of the heavens and over the livestock and over all the earth and over every creeping thing that creeps on the earth."
>
> 27 So God created man in his own image, in the image of God he created him; male and female he created them.
>
> 28 And God blessed them. And God said to them, "Be fruitful and multiply and fill the earth and subdue it and have dominion over the fish of the sea and over the birds of the heavens and over every living thing that moves on the earth."

Woman, just like man, was created in the image of God, given dominion over other creatures, and commanded to be fruitful and multiply. In fact, God considered the first man and woman to be so much alike that God called them both Adam (Gen. 5:2).

Despite this, the place of woman in creation has often been misunderstood. Some have viewed woman as an afterthought, even though the language of Genesis 1:26 indicates God's clear intention of creating more than one person before creating humanity.

Others suppose that the manner in which woman was created (out of the man's rib) gives her a derivative image of God. They argue that man is the image of God and that woman partakes in this image through submission to man. But this is a gross error. The Bible plainly teaches that there is only one mediator between humanity and God, and that is Jesus Christ (1 Tim. 2:5). Any suggestion that men are able to act as intermediaries between women and God robs Jesus of His rightful place as God's *only* mediator.[1]

Some have suggested that the description of Seth as bearing the image of Adam (Gen. 5:3) indicates that children also derive their image of God from men. But this is flatly contradicted by the birth of Jesus, who is the image of God (2 Cor. 4:4) and who was born to a virgin woman. Jesus' birth plainly indicated that the image of God does not require males for its existence or perpetuation.

As for what the image of Adam signifies, it could have been Adam's physical appearance or it could have been a reference to the sinful nature, of which Adam alone is held responsible, though both he and Eve sinned (Rom. 5:12).

We must be careful not to understand the image of God as being primarily comprised of physical attributes, including gender. Jesus taught that God is Spirit (John 4:24) and that

The Image of God

spirits do not have flesh and bones (Luke 24:39). This does not mean that our flesh is not part of the image of God—Jesus is, after all, the Word made flesh (John 1:14). God also specifically noted that to physically kill another human being is to destroy the image of God (Gen. 9:6).

But we must be careful of focusing on our physical bodies as the most important part of God's image when our bodies are made of dust (Gen. 2:7), will return to the ground (Gen. 3:14), and will one day be replaced with a new body (Rom. 8:23).

A Helper, But Not the Kind You Think

Another issue surrounding women in creation is the notion that woman was created *only* for man, with no purpose or responsibility apart from him. Many well-meaning Christians hold the view that women are "helpmeets" or "helpmates" for men. But the Bible's description of the first woman is as a helper that is comparable:

> **Genesis 2:18**
>
> **Then the LORD God said, "It is not good that the man should be alone; I will make him a helper fit for him."**

The Hebrew word that we translate into "help" or "helper" is *ezer*, and does not imply any notion of subordination or inferiority. The word translated "meet" or "fit" is *kenegdo*, meaning suitable, or comparable. The woman was suitable for man—not unsuitable.

A brief study of the usage of the word *ezer* indicates that it has a wide range of use in the Old Testament. Sometimes, it is used to refer to God as a "helper" of His people:

> **Isaiah 50:9**
>
> Behold, the Lord GOD helps me; who will declare me guilty? Behold, all of them will wear out like a garment; the moth will eat them up.

Other times *ezer* describes men helping others:

> **Joshua 1:14**
>
> Your wives, your little ones, and your livestock shall remain in the land that Moses gave you beyond the Jordan, but all the men of valor among you shall pass over armed before your brothers and shall help them,

And angels:

> **Daniel 10:13**
>
> The prince of the kingdom of Persia withstood me twenty-one days, but Michael, one of the chief princes, came to help me, for I was left there with the kings of Persia,

In the New Testament, Jesus describes a similar concept, though not linked through the Hebrew word *ezer*: the Holy Spirit as the Helper:

> **John 14:26**
>
> But the Helper, the Holy Spirit, whom the Father will send in my name, he will teach you all things and bring to your remembrance all that I have said to you.

As you can see from these verses, being a helper does not imply subordination or inferiority when used in reference to God, men, or angels. So it does not imply inferiority when it is used to describe women, either.

The Fall

The fall of the first man and woman into sin impaired the image of God in humanity, but did not destroy it (Gen. 9:6). But the consequences of their sin were severe, and included death (Gen. 3:19; Rom. 5:12; 6:23), universal condemnation of humanity (Rom. 5:18), power struggles in marital relationships (Gen. 3:16), additional pain in childbearing (Gen. 3:16), hatred between the serpent (Satan) and the woman (3:15), and all other kinds of evil. Through the fall sin entered the world (Rom. 5:12).

The impact of the fall on women has been the subject of much debate and discussion. Often, discussions of the fall are critical towards women and have negatively impacted perceptions of women generally, and in ministry.

Cause of the Fall

Some believe that women are the cause of the fall and view the woman as a seducer or temptress, but the Scriptures teach otherwise. The serpent is the one who is described as crafty and a deceiver (Gen. 3:1; 2 Cor. 11:3). Also, in the narrative, both the man and woman had some responsibility for the fall.

Consider: the man knew what God commanded and listened to the woman—even though he knew the serpent was lying (Gen. 3:17; 1 Tim. 2:14); the woman, while not hearing the original command, knew enough about it to avoid the tree, but didn't. When the serpent spoke to them, the two were already standing so close to the tree that they only had to stretch forth their hands to eat of it (Gen. 3:6). Why were they both standing so close to the forbidden tree?

There is much we do not know about this story, but to blame only the woman for the fall is like the religious leaders bringing only the woman caught in adultery to Jesus (John 8:3–11), as if she was alone when they found her. Jesus refused to condemn the woman then, and directed her accusers to consider their own sin. Before we condemn the woman for the fall of humanity, let us do likewise. We don't know everything about the fall, but we do know that the woman wasn't the only one at fault (Rom. 5:12–14; 2 Cor. 11:13).

Impact on Relationships

The fall impacted many different types of relationships, including the one between God and humanity (Gen. 3:9–13), the serpent (Satan) and humanity (Gen. 3:15), those between humans (Gen. 3:12,16), humanity and animals (Gen. 3:16), and humanity and the earth (3:17–19).

There is a range of perspectives on how the fall impacted male–female relationships. One fairly prevalent view among Christians is that God's statements after the fall are an expression God's will for male–female interaction. Since this is a view that is often related to the issue of women in ministry, we'll address it here.

First, God was not expressing His will for how marital relationships should function in Gen. 3:15, He was telling the woman what the consequences of her sin would be—the strife and power struggles within marriages.[2] God did not command Adam to rule over Eve; both of them were given dominion over the animals (Gen. 1:26–28). But they were not given dominion over each other after the fall. Rather, the entrance of sin into the world led to the attempts of husbands and wives (and everyone else in different relationships) to misplace that dominion by trying to dominate each other (Gen. 3:16). This dominating behavior is not sanctioned by God, it is a consequence of sin.

Second, all male–female interaction is not modeled on marital relationships. The Word of God provides many different examples of male–female interactions and they are not based on the fall or marriage. Examples include co-laborers for the gospel (Rom. 16:1), diplomatic interaction between queens and kings from different countries (2 Chr. 9:1–12), businesswomen and customers (Prov. 31:16; Acts 16:14–15), Queens and male servants (Acts 8:27–28), midwives and kings (Exod. 1:15–22), and plenty of others.

It is an error to suppose that all male–female relationships resemble marriage, and an even worse mistake to suppose that the fall renders women subordinate to men, either in marriage or generally. This was never God's design.

The Salvation of Jesus Christ
Finally, we cannot study the fall and its consequences to women without considering the salvation and restoration Jesus Christ provided for humanity, and its impact on women. Jesus Christ was manifested to destroy Satan's works (1 John 3:8), including all evil that resulted from the fall. Believes are now under the authority of Jesus Christ, not Satan.

Everyone who accepts Jesus as their Lord is "born again" (John 3:3) and becomes a "new creation" in Christ (2 Cor. 5:17). We are no longer slaves to sin (Rom. 6:6), but have God's Holy Spirit living in us (1 Cor. 6:19; 2 Tim. 1:14). In this newness of life, we do not have to struggle for power in any of our relationships. Rather we are commanded to love and serve others as Christ loved and served us (John 13:12–15,34). The sacrifice of Christ for His people is the model for Church leadership and for all male–female relationships. Not the fall.

Honoring the Image of God
Women are made in the image of God, so treating them as inferior to men or rejecting them from leadership because of their gender is showing disrespect to the God who created them. Even differences among humanity such as the rich and

poor are to be respected, because God is their creator (Prov. 22:2). This argument applies equally to women.

In Matthew 22, Jesus addressed this issue when responding to the Pharisees' attempt to trap Him. The immediate situation involved paying taxes. But Jesus also made some points that relate to the image of God:

> Matthew 22:15–22
>
> 15 Then the Pharisees went and plotted how to entangle him in his words.
>
> 16 And they sent their disciples to him, along with the Herodians, saying, "Teacher, we know that you are true and teach the way of God truthfully, and you do not care about anyone's opinion, for you are not swayed by appearances.
>
> 17 Tell us, then, what you think. Is it lawful to pay taxes to Caesar, or not?"
>
> 18 But Jesus, aware of their malice, said, "Why put me to the test, you hypocrites?
>
> 19 Show me the coin for the tax." And they brought him a denarius.
>
> 20 And Jesus said to them, "Whose likeness and inscription is this?"
>
> 21 They said, "Caesar's." Then he said to them, "Therefore render to Caesar the things that are Caesar's, and to God the things that are God's."
>
> 22 When they heard it, they marveled. And they left him and went away.

When the religious leaders asked Jesus about paying taxes to Caesar, Jesus showed them the image of Caesar on the coin for the tax, linking the image of Caesar and the requirements that were due him. In other words, the recognition of Caesar was directly tied to the treatment of his image. Pay taxes, honor Caesar. Refuse to pay taxes, dishonor Caesar.

But Jesus didn't end His statement there. He then noted the necessity of rendering to God the things due to God. Why?

The Image of God

Because the image of God was standing right in front of them (John 14:9; 2 Cor. 4:4; Col. 1:15). They were religious leaders, but did not know that Christ was God in the flesh (John 1:1–3; 2 Cor. 5:19) and that their treatment of Him (the image of God) was directly tied to their treatment of God. Those who honor Jesus are Honoring God; those who dishonor Jesus, dishonor God (Luke 12:8; John 13:20).

In everyday life, we come across instances of this principle. A working mother having a hectic day at work notices a picture of her smiling children on her desk. She smiles, briefly kisses the photo and thinks about how she will see them later that day. The love that she has for her children is demonstrated by her treatment of her kids' image in the photo. When she arrives home, her affection for her children is confirmed as she greets each one of them with a warm hug.

Here's another example: in a country filled with civil unrest and fighting, protesters have taken to the streets. A mini–mob gathers together, seeking a way to express their rage at the corruption of the government. As they turn down a side street they notice a poster of the current Prime Minister. In anger, they deface the poster with spray paint and throw bottles against it, breaking the bottles and shredding the poster. What do you think this mob would do if they got their hands on the Prime Minister? Just what they did to the poster—they would harm him.

The way we treat the image of a thing is the way we treat the thing itself. For too long the Church has neglected to understand that women are also the image of God. When women are dishonored and viewed as inferior this is not obedience to the Scriptures. Rather, those who dishonor women are actually dishonoring God, who created them.

NOTES

1. Similarly, teachings that suggest that a man is the priest of the Christian home are positioning the husband as a mediator between the family and God. Again, this robs Jesus of His rightful place as the *only* mediator between humanity and God. Husbands and wives may intercede for one another, but it is not necessary for either of them to "represent" God in the home—because God is living with them (John 14:23).

2. The Hebrew makes this point even more clearly, indicating that the woman shall desire to master her husband and that he will dominate her. In Genesis 4:7, the same language is used to describe the struggle between Cain and sin. This is not language of hierarchy, it's language that signifies a power struggle.

CHAPTER FOUR
Christ and His Followers

"Soon afterward [Jesus] went on through cities and villages, proclaiming and bringing the good news of the kingdom of God. And the twelve were with him, and also some women..."

LUKE 8:1–2

The incarnation, birth, life, ministry, and resurrection of Christ are among the best arguments in favor of women in ministry. Each of these aspects of Christ's existence lends support to the view that women are fundamentally equal to men and that God calls and equips women for ministry and leadership roles.

Even before Christ's incarnation, God revealed the birth and purpose of Christ to women. The angel Gabriel announced Christ's birth first to Mary, who was to be Christ's mother. The angel told her what her son was to be named (Jesus), that He would be the Son of God, that God would give Him the throne of David, and that His kingdom would be everlasting (Luke 1:26–38).

Later, Mary went to visit her cousin Elizabeth. When Elizabeth heard her voice, she was filled with the Holy Spirit and prophesied to Mary, referring to Christ as the Lord and confirming the fulfillment of the Lord's promise to Mary (Luke 1:39–45).

So the conception and birth of Christ did not involve any men, only God and a woman (Luke 1:35). That alone should give us pause. God, when providing salvation for humanity, worked with only a woman as His partner. We shouldn't think that God was forced to do this because of the manner in which children are born. As John the Baptist noted, God can raise up people from stones, if He chooses (Luke 3:8). God's choice of Mary was a sovereign decision that clearly demonstrates God's willingness to allow a woman to carry the Word, labor with the Word, and bring forth the Word. Jesus is, of course, the eternally existent Word of God.

God has evidenced His embracing of women in the most important aspects of Christ's life, including His incarnation, ministry, gospel, death, burial, and resurrection.

Christ, a Hebrew Man

In chapter 2, I discussed how Christians selectively view Christ's identity and focus on His maleness while ignoring His Jewishness, which has important implications on women in ministry. I will briefly reiterate that argument here.

Some Christians use Christ's identity to argue that women are not qualified to hold leadership roles in the Church. But, as noted earlier, Christ's maleness is not proof of male superiority over females generally or in the Church, any more than His Hebrew heritage is proof of Jewish superiority to Gentiles in the Church.

Christ was prophesied to be a Hebrew male—the seed of Abraham and the Son of David (Gen. 5:15; Matt. 1:1; Gal. 3:16). So we must consider both of those aspects of Christ's earthly identity when working to understand what it means for Church leadership.

If we apply the arguments typically used to disqualify women from Church leadership, they also disqualify Gentiles. Christ came as a Hebrew, and all of the 12 apostles were Hebrew (Acts 2:7). In the Old Testament, the entire priesthood was Hebrew (Exod. 28:1; Lev. 21:1). Does anyone interpret this to mean that only Hebrews can lead in the Church? No.

So if the fact that Christ, the apostles, the prophets, and all the Old Testament priests were Hebrew doesn't exclude Gentiles from Church leadership, then the fact that Christ, the apostles and the Old Testament priests were male does not exclude women from Church leadership, either.

Christ existed as the Word of God from all eternity (John 1:1). His taking on of human flesh was part of God's plan to save His people (Matt. 1:21; 1 Tim. 3:16). Nothing in the New Testament indicates that the advent of Christ was a statement by God as to the superiority of any ethnic group or gender.

The Early Church

Many Christians are not aware that the distinction between Jews and Gentiles was significant in the early Church, but it was. In fact, not long after the Day of Pentecost, a dispute arose as to whether Gentiles could even be saved.

In Acts 10, an angel visited a Gentile named Cornelius and instructed him to summon Peter to his house to hear Peter's message. In preparation for this visit, the Holy Spirit gave Peter a vision to tell him to go with Cornelius' servants—otherwise Peter wouldn't have gone. As a strict observer of the Law, he would not have eaten with Gentiles, because their food would have been unclean to him (Acts 10:14).

Peter went to Cornelius' house, heard about Cornelius' vision of the angel and realized that God had provided salvation to the Gentiles. How? Because while he preached to them about salvation in Christ, the Holy Spirit fell on the Gentiles and they began to speak with other tongues just as the first believers had (Acts 10:44–46).

But the rest of Christ's followers didn't realize what had happened and when Peter returned to Jerusalem, they were angry with him for spending time with Gentiles (Acts 11:1–3). Once Peter explained that the Holy Spirit had fallen on the Gentiles, Christ's Hebrew followers realized that God had provided salvation to the Gentiles. But they were surprised—they apparently hadn't thought that Gentiles could be saved.[1]

In the Old Testament, there are plenty of verses that suggest that God had plans for Gentiles that included salvation, starting with the fact that Abraham was uncircumcised when called by God (Gen. 17:10–27; Rom. 4:9–10). The inclusion of Rahab, a woman from Jericho, in the lineage of Christ is another example. Another is the provision in the Law for strangers to join Israel (Num. 15:14–16). Or that Ruth, a Moabite, was King David's grandmother. Even the prophecies of salvation for Ethiopa and Egypt point to a broad plan of salvation (Ps. 68:31; Isa. 11:19–25). Not to mention the miracles Jesus performed and His interaction with Gentiles (Matt. 15:21–28; Luke 7:1–10; John 4:7–42).

But the Jewish identity of Christ and His followers led the early Church to believe that salvation was strictly for Jews—until God showed them otherwise. When we discuss Christ's identity, we must understand that the Hebrew aspect of His identity was central to who He was and not something to be ignored. It is just as important as His maleness.

So those arguing that Christ's gender is the model for Church leadership must also argue that his ethnic heritage is the model for Church leadership. These two aspects of His identity are intertwined: Christ is not just a "Son," He is the Son of David and the Seed of Abraham. He is a Hebrew Son. Christ is also God—the eternally existent Son of God.

The Ministry and Teachings of Jesus

Jesus' interaction with and ministry to women provides another illustration of His acceptance of women and His belief in their equality to men and their leadership abilities. Jesus' treatment of women was a major departure from the culture of His day.

Throughout the Gospels, Jesus spent considerable time with women; they were among His most dedicated followers:

Christ and His Followers

> **Luke 8:1–3**
>
> 1 Soon afterward he went on through cities and villages, proclaiming and bringing the good news of the kingdom of God. And the twelve were with him,
>
> 2 and also some women who had been healed of evil spirits and infirmities: Mary, called Magdalene, from whom seven demons had gone out,
>
> 3 and Joanna, the wife of Chuza, Herod's household manager, and Susanna, and many others, who provided for them out of their means.

Not only did these women support Jesus financially (v. 3), they followed Him all the way to His crucifixion (Matt. 27:55–56; Luke 23:49) even visiting His tomb (Matt. 27:61; Luke 23:55–24:3). They were present at His ascension and He baptized them in the Holy Spirit on the Day of Pentecost (Acts 1:8–15).

These women followed Christ for a variety of reasons, but part of His appeal to them was in the content of His teachings, which showcased Christ's (and God's) rejection of human traditions that oppressed women. An example of this occurred in Matthew 19, where the religious leaders asked Christ about divorce:

> **Matthew 19:3–6**
>
> 3 And Pharisees came up to him and tested him by asking, 'Is it lawful to divorce one's wife for any cause?'
>
> 4 He answered, 'Have you not read that he who created them from the beginning made them male and female,
>
> 5 and said, 'Therefore a man shall leave his father and his mother and hold fast to his wife, and the two shall become one flesh'?
>
> 6 So they are no longer two but one flesh. What therefore God has joined together, let not man separate."

The Pharisees' question about divorce was a loaded one. It highlights the (seemingly) male prerogative of divorce that was in the Law (Deut. 24:1). In some ways it was also a test of Jesus' allegiance—did He support the men or the women on the issue? The religious leaders also saw the support Jesus received from women, and may have hoped to erode it.

But as Jesus' response made clear, His allegiance was to God, who created man and woman. By pointing out that God created men and women (Matt. 19:4) and the institution of marriage (Matt. 19:6), Jesus was reminding the religious leaders of God's concern with how women are treated generally, and within the institution of marriage.

Jesus' ministry also reflected His view of women as equals. In John 4, He conversed at length with a Samaritan woman at a well, a move which astonished His disciples (John 4:27). He talked with her about politics (the disagreement between the Jews and Samaritans) and religion (the proper place to worship God), which was not commonly done. At the conclusion of their conversation, He revealed Himself to her as the Messiah (John 4:25–26).

This was no ordinary woman. She had been married five times and was currently living with a man she wasn't married to (John 4:16–18). Consider for a moment how persuasive this woman was. She had married and divorced *five* different men and convinced a sixth man to live with her—in a culture where women were treated as subordinates! She was also perfectly comfortable discussing her opinion with Christ.

It isn't altogether surprising to see that she was an influential person in her community. When she went into town and told the people about Christ, they followed her out to the well and many believed because of her testimony (John 4:39). Many more believed after hearing Christ (John 4:42). But the result was that salvation came to a community in part because of this woman. God used her efforts for His glory.

Christ and His Followers

In addition to talking with women He encountered in ministry, Jesus also allowed women to learn from Him in the same manner as His male disciples:

> Luke 10:38–42
>
> **38** Now as they went on their way, Jesus entered a village. And a woman named Martha welcomed him into her house.
>
> **39** And she had a sister called Mary, who sat at the Lord's feet and listened to his teaching.
>
> **40** But Martha was distracted with much serving. And she went up to him and said, "Lord, do you not care that my sister has left me to serve alone? Tell her then to help me."
>
> **41** But the Lord answered her, "Martha, Martha, you are anxious and troubled about many things,
>
> **42** but one thing is necessary. Mary has chosen the good portion, which will not be taken away from her."

The contrast between the actions of Martha and Mary figures prominently in this story. Martha is busy serving and is annoyed that her sister Mary was sitting at Jesus' feet, learning.

There are several things to notice about this story. First, Mary was sitting at Jesus' feet, a posture adopted by disciples of a teacher (Acts 22:3).[2] Further, Jesus affirmed Mary's choice and her right to be in the position of a disciple; He had no expectation that Mary would fulfill a traditional woman's role, even in her sister's house.

Martha, despite her incorrect focus, demonstrated the intimacy of her relationship with Jesus—she felt comfortable enough with Him to complain about Mary and His response to Mary's conduct. But Martha also exemplifies the response that many women have when they encounter other women in ministry: they desire to force women ministers back into traditional women's roles.

But that's not the end of Martha's story. Later in the Gospel of John, she found herself on the receiving end of divine revelation. The revelation of Christ to Martha provides further evidence of God's willingness to reveal His mysteries and secrets to women:

> John 11:25–27
>
> 25 Jesus said to her, "I am the resurrection and the life. Whoever believes in me, though he die, yet shall he live,
>
> 26 and everyone who lives and believes in me shall never die. Do you believe this?"
>
> 27 She said to him, "Yes, Lord; I believe that you are the Christ, the Son of God, who is coming into the world."

In verse 27, Martha acknowledges Jesus as the Christ and the Son of God, a revelation also given to Peter (Matt. 16:16–17). You have probably heard that Peter received a revelation about Jesus as the Christ. How many times have you heard that Martha received this revelation from God?[3]

The miracles of Jesus demonstrated God's compassion toward women. In the synagogue, He healed a woman who was bowed over with a spirit of illness for 18 years and rebuked the religious leaders for their bias against her (Luke 13:10–17).

In another instance, a woman who had a discharge of blood for 12 years touched Christ and was made whole (Mark 5:25–34). What's remarkable about this story is that the woman was considered unclean under the Law—*for all twelve years of her condition* (Lev. 15:25). Anyone touching her would be considered unclean, so her condition had the effect of keeping her separate from the rest of the community. But Jesus showed no displeasure at her touch and His healing restored her to the community. It also pointed to God's unwillingness to see women ostracized because of female bodily functions.

Girls also benefitted from Jesus' healing power. After healing the woman with the issue of blood, Jesus continued going towards the house of Jairus, the ruler of the synagogue, whose daughter was ill. When he arrived, he healed her, and restored her to her family. As a daughter, some in the community may not have viewed her as important, but God desired for her to be well. There are other instances of Jesus healing women and girls in the Gospels, but these examples will at least give you a sense of how Christ's ministry impacted women.

Christ's Death, Burial and Resurrection

The close relationship between Jesus and women was highlighted even in His death, burial and resurrection. Shortly before Jesus died, a woman anointed Him with oil in preparation for His burial (Mark 14:8). The disciples thought her action was a waste, but Jesus appreciated her gift and linked the preaching of the gospel (His story) to her story (Mark 14:9). In defending the woman, Jesus observed: "She has done what she could." (Mark 14:8) Women must understand that we are expected to do whatever we can for Christ, even if His male disciples disapprove.

The biblical narratives surrounding Jesus' death also prominently feature women, starting at the cross:

> **John 19:25-27**
>
> **25 but standing by the cross of Jesus were his mother and his mother's sister, Mary the wife of Clopas, and Mary Magdalene.**
>
> **26 When Jesus saw his mother and the disciple whom he loved standing nearby, he said to his mother, "Woman, behold, your son!"**
>
> **27 Then he said to the disciple, "Behold, your mother!" And from that hour the disciple took her to his own home.**

We would expect Jesus' mother to be nearby during His crucifixion, but there were other women present who had accompanied Him from Galilee—these women were Christ's followers (Matt. 27:55-56; Mark 15:40-41; Luke 23:49).

Another aspect of Christ's crucifixion that relates to women is often overlooked. In verses 26 and 27, when Jesus spoke to His mother and the disciple with her, He was, in one sense, expressing His will that the disciple care for her. But His words also contained a much more profound message.

The phrase "Woman, behold your son!" has an additional meaning that is related to Genesis 3:15, where God told the serpent (Satan):

Genesis 3:15

I will put enmity between you and the woman, and between your offspring and her offspring; he shall bruise your head, and you shall bruise his heel."

At first glance, there may not seem to be a connection between Jesus' death on the cross and this verse. But let's take a closer look.

We already know that Jesus is the offspring of the woman. He was born of Mary, a virgin (Luke 1:26-38; 2:7); He is the *woman's* seed. The serpent (Satan) had already bruised His heel. How do we know? Because in the Bible, the heel signifies betrayal (Ps. 41:9; John 13:18). Like when Jacob held the heel of his brother Esau at their birth, and later betrayed him (Gen. 25:26; 27:35-36).

Judas, possessed by Satan (Luke 22:3; John 13:27), betrayed Jesus—that's when the serpent bruised Jesus' heel. This left only one remaining action that needed to occur in order to complete Genesis 3:15: the woman's offspring (Jesus) had to bruise the head of the serpent, which Jesus

Christ and His Followers

accomplished through His death and resurrection (Col. 2:12-15).

So when Jesus said "Woman, behold your son!" He was also saying "Woman, behold your seed!" signifying His role in God's redemptive plan for humanity. Jesus' statement is even more poignant when you realize that He said it while dying on a cross, soon to be buried in the ground—like a seed (John 12:23-24).

After Jesus died, Mary Magdalene and another Mary went to the grave where Jesus' body was put, and sat there (Matt. 27:61; Mark 15:47; 27:55-56). They loved Him and wished to be near Him. God did not include the stories of these women in His Word for no reason; the Scripture was written for our learning (Rom. 5:14). These women were devoted to Christ, remaining faithful even after His death. Is there a more important qualification for ministry and leadership among God's people?

The next day, the two Marys went back to Jesus' grave with spices and perfumes to anoint His body. Instead, they found angels who sent them to the disciples (Matt. 28:1-7; Mark 16:1-8; Luke 24:1-11). As they went, Jesus appeared to them and sent them with a message for the disciples (Matt. 28:8-10; Mark 16:9-11). Jesus first appeared after His resurrection to a woman, Mary Magdalene (John 20:11–18).

Women in the Early Church

After Christ's resurrection and ascension, women continued to be active in the early Church, but their involvements and contributions are often glossed over and sometimes completely dismissed. By examining their efforts we get a glimpse into God's work through women in the early Church.

Before Christ's ascension into heaven, He instructed His followers to wait in Jerusalem for the Holy Spirit. The group that waited included the twelve apostles, the women who followed Christ and many others. We know this because on the day of Pentecost there were 120 people gathered together in one place (Acts 1:9–14; 2:1–4).

Then Jesus baptized all of them—men and women—in the Holy Spirit:

> Acts 2:1–4
>
> **1 When the day of Pentecost arrived, they were all together in one place.**
>
> **2 And suddenly there came from heaven a sound like a mighty rushing wind, and it filled the entire house where they were sitting.**
>
> **3 And divided tongues as of fire appeared to them and rested on each one of them.**
>
> **4 And they were all filled with the Holy Spirit and began to speak in other tongues as the Spirit gave them utterance.**

There is considerable significance to women's participation in the Day of Pentecost. They were not just present as observers or tag-alongs, but were part of Joel's prophecy that was being fulfilled:

> Acts 2:14–18
>
> **14 But Peter, standing with the eleven, lifted up his voice and addressed them: "Men of Judea and all who dwell in Jerusalem, let this be known to you, and give ear to my words.**
>
> **15 For these people are not drunk, as you suppose, since it is only the third hour of the day.**
>
> **16 But this is what was uttered through the prophet Joel:**
>
> **17 "'And in the last days it shall be, God declares, that I will pour out my Spirit on all flesh, and your sons and your daughters shall prophesy, and your young men shall see visions, and your old men shall dream dreams;**
>
> **18 even on my male servants and female servants in those days I will pour out my Spirit, and they shall prophesy.**

God poured out His Spirit upon humanity without regard to human-made distinctions. Men and women were included in the outpouring, along with sons and daughters, and masters and servants. God's Word specifically included both genders across age groups and social status.

The Holy Spirit is a gift (Luke 11:13; Acts 2:38; 10:45) who empowers Christian believers for service to God. This same Holy Spirit also distributes gifts to those who believe on Christ—not in accordance with their gender, or human notions of male and female roles, but in accordance with the will of God (Heb. 2:4).

The challenges facing the early Church also revealed women as having some leadership roles:

Acts 8:3

But Saul was ravaging the church, and entering house after house, he dragged off men and women and committed them to prison.

On the surface, the fact that men and women were imprisoned would not seem particularly noteworthy. But those jailed for the cause of Christ were generally leaders—people known to authorities and whose imprisonment would discourage or hinder God's work. That women were imprisoned for the cause of Christ shows their value to the community. Jesus specifically cited such trials as a great honor (Matt. 5:11–12; Luke 21:12–15).

Christ, Our High Priest

One other aspect of Christ's present-day ministry has implications for women in ministry: His role as the High Priest of believers. A full examination of the doctrine of Christ as High Priest is beyond the scope of this book, but several parts of it relates to the issue of women in ministry.

God's oath making Christ a High Priest apart from the requirements of the Law is a prominent example of God's sovereignty when it comes to selecting religious leaders for His people. Under the Law, the priesthood was reserved for descendants of Aaron, who was of the tribe of Levi (Exod. 28:1, Num. 3:10-13). But Jesus was a descendant of the tribe of Judah, a group not designated as priests. He became a High Priest because God, in His sovereign power, changed the priesthood (Ps. 110:4). This doesn't mean that God violated His Word, because God had already provided an example of this priesthood in Melchizedek (Gen. 14:17-20).[4]

Jesus' selection as High Priest is similar in some ways to the story of Cornelius and the Gentiles in Acts 10. The early Church didn't realize that God had extended salvation to the Gentiles and were surprised when it happened. But God had signified early in the Word His intention to save Gentiles (Gen. 12:1-3; Deut. 32:43); it was the Church that hadn't made the connection. In the case of Jesus and the salvation of the Gentiles, God foreshadowed the event and performed it while the Church struggled to understand what happened.[5]

One other issue related to Jesus' role as High Priest has to do with the importance of Melchizedek, the ancient priest. This man was no ordinary priest, for when God made Jesus a High Priest, He did so with this oath: "You are a priest forever after the order of Melchizedek." (Ps. 110:4) This gives us some idea of the ancient priest's importance! The author of Hebrews described Melchizedek as greater than Abraham (Heb. 7:7) and noted that Abraham paid tithes to him (Gen. 14:20), and that he (Melchizedek) blessed Abraham (Gen. 14:19).

For someone so important, the Bible provides us with virtually no information about Melchizedek—no genealogy, no birth or death information. Only a brief interaction with Abraham (then Abram) (Gen. 14:17-20) and a discussion of that interlude in Hebrews.

So what does this have to with women in ministry?

One line of arguments against women in ministry views the women leaders in the Bible as less significant because they are fewer in number, and because there is less information about them than the male leaders in the Bible. But the story of Melchizedek helps us to understand that a person's importance to God is not determined by the length or detail of their biblical account. The Bible gives us no genealogy for Melchizedek, nor do we know how he became a priest. We have very little information about him—yet he was greater than Abraham. His brief appearance does not negate his value.

And so it is with women in ministry. The stories of Miriam, Deborah, Huldah, Anna, Martha, Priscilla, and Phoebe may not be as lengthy or as detailed as those of the more prominent men, but this does not signify that these women's callings or efforts were any less important to God. The Bible's very short stories, like that of Melchizedek, involve people whose ministries are of great value to God.

NOTES

1. Dr. George O. Wood has written an article that argues that the model of inclusion for Gentiles in the early Church could also be used to include women in ministry. While I am using Acts 10 primarily to confirm the importance of Christ's Jewish identity to early believers, Dr. Wood's article provides a more direct link between the inclusion of Gentiles in the faith and women in ministry. See Wood, George. O. "Exploring Why We Think the Way We Do About Women in Ministry," *Enrichment Journal 1* (2001): 9-14.

2. Some believe that Mary's sitting position at Jesus' feet as a disciple could signify that she would later have greater teaching opportunities, as did Paul after sitting at the feet of Gamaliel (Acts 22:3).

3. Jesus' reference to the "rock" upon which the Church is built is not Peter—a sinful person like everyone else. Rather, the rock is the revelation that Jesus is the Christ, the Son of the Living God. Jesus didn't tell Peter the Church would be built on him (Peter), but upon the revelation.

4. I am indebted to Jordan May for this point.

5. See note 1, above.

CHAPTER FIVE
Understanding First Timothy

"[Paul's] letters contain some things that are hard to understand, which ignorant and unstable people distort, as they do the other Scriptures, to their own destruction."

2 PETER 3:16

Most of the arguments against women in ministry center on a portion of First Timothy 2 that has been widely misunderstood and misinterpreted. In this chapter, we'll examine the verses at the center of the controversy and discuss their implications for women in ministry. Let's start by reading the Word:

> **1 Timothy 2:11–15**
>
> **11 Let a woman learn quietly with all submissiveness.**
>
> **12 I do not permit a woman to teach or to exercise authority over a man; rather, she is to remain quiet.**
>
> **13 For Adam was formed first, then Eve;**
>
> **14 and Adam was not deceived, but the woman was deceived and became a transgressor.**
>
> **15 Yet she will be saved through childbearing—if they continue in faith and love and holiness, with self-control.**

The traditional argument against women in ministry interprets verses 13–15 to mean that God wants only men in positions of authority, because: men were formed first (v.13), and the first woman was deceived (v.14). Part three of the argument suggests that God wants women to focus on their families (v.15). There are some variations on this argument, but this is the essence of it.

The problem with this argument is that it completely misunderstands Paul's point. Many Christians believe that Paul was referring to creation to show the universality of male leadership. But that isn't what Paul was doing. He was referencing the events which took place to illustrate a parallel to the situation confronting Timothy.

The chart below illustrates the parallel between Paul's argument and the creation accounts:

1 Tim. 2:13–15	Genesis 1–3
Adam was first formed then Eve (2:13)	Creation of humanity (1:26,27; 2:7-8, 18-23)
The woman was deceived; the man was not (2:14)	The fall of humanity (3:1-7)
Woman will be saved through childbearing (2:15)	The promise of redemption (3:15)

It is obvious from Paul's reference to creation that this is a much greater issue than whether women can lead in Church. What Paul is discussing has to do with the creation and fall of humanity and the promise of redemption.

Part 1: The Order of Creation

Let's start with the order of creation. The first part of Paul's argument has been misinterpreted to mean that the person created first is the one that God intends to have authority—or the one God regards as most important. The problem with this argument is that throughout the Old Testament, God often chose the person who was second, or even the youngest of many, to rule.

In the order of creation, animals were created first. Since human beings were created after them, does this make humans secondary to animals? Of course not. This is an obvious example of how we do not interpret the Bible to mean that first is better. Some would argue this point because human beings are made in the image of God, while animals are not.

So let's look at Cain and Abel. When Cain and Abel brought offerings to God, God accepted Abel's offering over Cain's. Abel was the younger brother; Cain was the first-born (Gen. 4:1–2). Again, some would dispute this point because Cain and Abel's offerings were accepted because of their content, not because of birth order.

What about Abraham's sons? Abraham had two sons: Ishmael, his first-born and Isaac, who was Abraham's second son (Gen. 17:15–21). Abraham's primary heir was Isaac, the second-born. God chose him and his children as the ones through whom the Messiah would come (Gen. 21:12). Some may argue that Isaac was Abraham's first son with Sarah—or the first one conceived within marriage. But they were both Abraham's sons and God chose the second-born over the first.

Later, Isaac had twins, Esau and Jacob, with his wife Rebekah. Esau was the first-born and Jacob was born second. But God chose Jacob (the younger) and his children as His people and rejected Esau (Gen. 25:23–26). It cannot be argued that God's choice was based on the conduct of the children, since God determined that Jacob was to be the younger and the chosen ruler before they were even born (Gen. 25:23; Rom. 9:11–13).

There are other examples of this, as well. When God wanted to preserve Israel's heritage, He sent Joseph ahead to be ruler over Egypt (Gen. 45:4–8). Joseph was the second-youngest son of Jacob. It was expected in their culture that the oldest should lead, so when Joseph had dreams about his brothers bowing down to him—and his parents—his brothers and even his father were angry (Gen. 37:5–11). It was unthinkable that he, almost the youngest, should rule over them. But that's exactly what happened (Gen. 42:6; 43:26).

When the prophet Samuel was sent by God to the house of Jesse to anoint one of his sons as king over Israel, Samuel thought that he was to anoint the first-born (1 Sam. 16:6; 17:13). As it turned out, God had chosen the youngest son (1 Sam. 16:11). Again, God chose the youngest to rule over those older than him.

There are plenty of other examples that prove that God often chooses the second over the first. The Apostle Paul knew all of this. He was a student of Gamaliel, a well-respected rabbi (Acts 22:3), and an Old Testament scholar. Paul was well-versed in the Jewish Scriptures. He wasn't making an argument about men having authority because they were chronologically first, because there are numerous examples where God chose those who were not chronologically first to lead.

So what did Paul mean? It's tied to the next verse. I'll explain more after we study verse 14.

Part 2: Easily Deceived?

In 1 Timothy 2:14, Paul continues his argument:

> **1 Timothy 2:14**
>
> **And Adam was not deceived, but the woman being deceived, fell into transgression.**

Some Christians understand this statement to mean that women cannot lead either because they are more easily deceived, or because the first woman was deceived. This is a gross misinterpretation of the Word of God, for a few reasons.

First, it is a fairly common, and major error to suppose that Eve is a type of all women, and that Adam is a type of all men. While it is true that their sinful nature passed along to all of humanity (Ps. 51:5; Rom. 5:12), there is nothing which indicates that sin is passed down by gender.

We read in the Bible of male and female murderers (Gen. 4:8; 1 Kgs. 18:13), liars (Acts 5:1–11), adulterers (Lev. 20:10) and every other kind of sin. The Law makes provision for men and women committing the same types of sins (Num. 5:6–7), which Christ affirmed (Mark 10:11–12).

There is also no indication that women are more easily deceived than men. The Bible provides examples of two men among Christ's apostles who were deceived and misled by Satan—Peter and Judas.

The first of Satan's efforts took place during a time when the Lord was describing His crucifixion to His disciples. After He finished, Peter took Jesus aside and rebuked Him, trying to tell the Lord that He would not be crucified:

> **Matthew 16:22–23**
>
> 22 And Peter took him aside and began to rebuke him, saying, "Far be it from you, Lord! This shall never happen to you."
>
> 23 But he turned and said to Peter, "Get behind me, Satan! You are a hindrance to me. For you are not setting your mind on the things of God, but on the things of man."

Jesus' response to Peter is instructive. He indicates plainly that Satan was influencing Peter's conduct (v. 23). Then, shortly before the Lord's crucifixion, Jesus told Peter that Satan wasn't finished with him yet:

> **Luke 22:31–32**
>
> 31 "Simon, Simon, behold, Satan demanded to have you, that he might sift you like wheat,
>
> 32 but I have prayed for you that your faith may not fail. And when you have turned again, strengthen your brothers."

Peter denied the Lord multiple times (Matt. 26:69–75; Luke 22:55–62), a behavior Christ foretold him would be influenced by Satan. As for Judas, the Bible teaches us that Satan actually entered into him (Luke 22:3; John 13:27). Being deceived by Satan is not limited to women, since even two of Christ's apostles, including Peter who was especially favored (Matt. 17:1–3), were misled and influenced by Satan.

The suggestion that God prevents women from leading because Eve was deceived is even more ridiculous—as if God is punishing all women because Eve sinned. If that's the case, then men are also prevented from leading because Adam, who was not deceived by the serpent, willfully sinned against God. Both of them sinned.

What Paul Meant

So what did Paul mean by verses 13–14? We've already discussed that God often chooses those that are second (or later in chronological order) to rule and lead, and we see that deception by Satan is not limited to women.

The way to understand what these verses mean is by looking at them together. Paul links the order in which the man and woman were created and the woman's deception, and this provides the key to understanding this passage. The creation account in Genesis 2 provides the answer:

> **Genesis 2:15–18, 21-22**
>
> **15** The Lord God took the man and put him in the garden of Eden to work it and keep it.
>
> **16** And the Lord God commanded the man, saying, "You may surely eat of every tree of the garden,
>
> **17** but of the tree of the knowledge of good and evil you shall not eat, for in the day that you eat of it you shall surely die."
>
> **18** Then the Lord God said, "It is not good that the man should be alone; I will make him a helper fit for him."...

> 21 So the Lord God caused a deep sleep to fall upon the man, and while he slept took one of his ribs and closed up its place with flesh.
>
> 22 And the rib that the Lord God had taken from the man he made into a woman and brought her to the man.

Consider the order of what took place: God created Adam, commanded him not to eat of the tree of the knowledge of good and evil, and then God created woman.

To clarify: God had not created the woman when He gave the command to Adam.

This is the reason that Paul juxtaposed the order of creation and the woman's deception in 1 Timothy 2. Because the order of creation provided an occasion for the woman to be deceived—because she wasn't around to hear the original command.

In Hebrew, the discussion between the woman and the serpent makes it clear that the serpent was aware of God's command, while the woman was not. First, let's read the English version and then I'll reference the Hebrew:

> **Genesis 3:1–4**
>
> 1 Now the serpent was more crafty than any other beast of the field that the LORD God had made. He said to the woman, "Did God actually say, 'You shall not eat of any tree in the garden'?"
>
> 2 And the woman said to the serpent, "We may eat of the fruit of the trees in the garden,
>
> 3 but God said, 'You shall not eat of the fruit of the tree that is in the midst of the garden, neither shall you touch it, lest you die.'"
>
> 4 But the serpent said to the woman, "You will not surely die.

In Hebrew, the woman's response to the serpent makes it obvious that she has not heard what God said. The words of her response do not resemble God's original statement, and she adds to God's statement. But the serpent's response to the woman negates what God has said using exactly the same language that God used with Adam. You can see in the Hebrew that the serpent has heard what God has said while the woman has not. In disputing God's command, the serpent repeats it precisely (and makes it plural for the man and woman), while the woman doesn't get it right at all.

Now we come to Paul's concern in 1 Timothy. Paul's statements were not a universal statement against women in leadership; he was observing the similarity between the position of women in the local congregation and the position in which Eve found herself in Genesis. Much has been written about the cultural context in which Paul lived when he wrote to Timothy. But the lens through which Paul wanted Timothy to understand his congregation's situation was Genesis, with particular reference to the relative knowledge of men and women at that time.

The similarity between Genesis and Timothy's congregation was this: both involved women who lacked direct, substantive knowledge of God's Word. In Timothy's culture, women were generally not a part of public discourse, and were not informed about the Word of God in the same way that men were, at least not initially. Eve, as we know from Genesis 2, lacked direct knowledge about God's command because she hadn't been created.

Paul's letter to Timothy seems to be partially in response to some women in the local congregation who had taken it upon themselves to teach without having knowledge and understanding of the Word. It is these women that Paul forbade to teach. The issue was not about them being women, rather Paul used the fact that women were involved to draw a parallel to the temptation and sin that befell Eve.

That deception was based not on her gender. It happened because she was not alive when God gave the command, resulting in her incomplete knowledge of God's command. The Genesis account does not tell us how Eve found out about the command or who told her. But whatever happened, she was eventually deceived by the serpent. Adam, who heard the command directly from God, was not (1 Tim. 2:14).

So Paul's message to Timothy was this: to allow unlearned women to teach would effectively place them in the same position as Eve was in—they would have had influence but not knowledge. This would make them susceptible (as Eve was) to temptation and sin. Not because they are women, but because of their lack of knowledge. In their current unlearned condition, these women would have jeopardized the well-being of the congregation by making place for Satan, the tempter.

This was not the first time Paul expressed concern that Satan be prevented from influencing the churches. In some instances, as in 1 Timothy 5, Paul reminded Timothy about the efforts of Satan to ensnare younger widows in the congregation (1 Tim. 5:9–16). In 1 Corinthians 7:5, he reminded the married couples at Corinth that Satan would seek to tempt them, and advised them to be on their guard. In 2 Corinthians 2:10–12, Paul discussed how forgiveness prevents Satan from gaining a foothold in the congregation.

Paul's reference to the woman's deception in 1 Timothy 2:14 also contained an implicit reference to and concern about Satan, the serpent of Genesis. Note that in Genesis, one consequence of the serpent's actions was that God put hatred between the serpent (Satan) and the woman, and between their offspring:

> **Genesis 3:15**
>
> I will put enmity between you and the woman, and between your offspring and her offspring; he shall bruise your head, and you shall bruise his heel."

So while Paul is drawing a parallel between the situation of unlearned women and Eve, he is also cautioning Timothy against putting women in a situation that will allow Satan to exploit their lack of knowledge.

The end result of Paul's teaching is that in situations or cultures where women (or men) are unlearned—that is, in the same position as Eve was in Genesis—they are not to teach. Not because of gender, but because having untaught people teach gives occasion to Satan to deceive and mislead them.

How does this impact women in ministry today? In many cultures, women are taught the Word of God and have the ability to learn. Under Paul's argument, there is no prohibition against such women teaching, because they are not in the same position as Eve—they have had a chance to learn and understand the Word of God.

Part 3: Childbearing and Salvation

The final verse of 1 Timothy 2 concludes Paul's argument:

> **1 Timothy 2:15**
>
> Yet she will be saved through childbearing—if they continue in faith and love and holiness, with self-control.

This third part of Paul's argument relates to the promise of salvation through the woman's offspring (Gen. 3:15). Paul is obviously not suggesting that women are saved through bearing children, since our salvation occurs by grace through faith in Christ (Eph. 2:8).

Paul, who advocated singleness in First Corinthians (1 Cor. 7:8), was also not suggesting that having a family and children is essential to salvation. What would such a suggestion mean for virgins, widows and those choosing to remain unmarried for the sake of Christ?

Rather, Paul is finishing his parallel to creation, reminding Timothy of the salvation in Christ that was promised and came through a woman (Gen. 3:15). He reminds Timothy that God often uses women to help achieve His purposes. This parallels some of God's other major deliverances that prominently feature women and the birth of a child who eventually leads God's people.

The story of Moses is full of women: the midwives that helped the Israelite women deliver children (Exod. 1:15–22), his older sister who stood guard over him (Exod. 2:4) and Pharaoh's daughter who adopted him (Exod. 2:6–10).

Samson's mother was visited by an angel who foretold the birth of her son (Judg. 13:2–5). When she told her husband, he prayed to God. God answered his prayer by sending the angel back to the woman (Judg. 13:9)! God dealt directly with Samson's mother and only spoke with her husband (Samson's father) when she brought him to where God was (Judg. 13:10–14).

Samuel was born to Hannah, a woman who was one of two wives. Hannah was barren and in her sorrow vowed to give her son to God (1 Sam. 1:1–20). Through her, and the women mentioned earlier, God was able to bring deliverance to His people. Paul is reminding Timothy of this fact.

Some have suggested that verse 15 is a command for women to tend to their families instead of teaching. I think that is a misunderstanding of verse 15. In 1 Timothy 5, Paul advises Timothy that younger widows should marry, but that is a different situation than the one Paul is addressing in 1 Timothy 2. And as we know from leaders like Deborah,

Huldah, and Priscilla, being married and ministering are not mutually exclusive.

* * *

We ought to pay more attention to Peter's statement that Paul's sayings are "hard to be understood." This same Peter received the revelation of Christ from God (Matt. 15:16-18) and saw Christ transfigured on the mount (Matt. 17:1-8). So if *he* is saying the Paul's writing can be hard to understand, we should not expect to easily interpret it. Paul was the recipient of great revelation, and his epistles are not understood by a superficial reading of the text. The Word of God does not yield its fruit easily and it is easy to misunderstand what has been written for our learning.

When Paul spoke of women in 1 Timothy 2, it was not a universal prohibition on women teaching or holding authority—it was a command designed to prevent unlearned people in the community from falling into the same situation as Eve. In ancient times, most such people in that position were women. Today, in many cultures, women have the same opportunities to learn the Word of God as men, so there is no special danger in women teaching or holding authority.

The lesson we need to glean from Paul's teaching is that those holding authority and teaching in the Church must be taught in the Word of God—not that leadership is determined on the basis of gender.

CHAPTER SIX
Human Tradition vs. God's Commands

"For laying aside the commandment of God, you hold the tradition of men..."

MATTHEW 15:6

One of the more common arguments against women in ministry is tradition. Traditions are customs, behaviors, or beliefs that have been passed down through generations. In the Church, traditions are often viewed as divinely ordained, even when not specifically supported by the Bible. Tradition is powerful: it is rooted in the history of human interactions, and when those interactions become commonplace in the Church, they are often understood as being the will of God—even when they're not.

Tradition has had a significant impact on the treatment of women in Christianity, including women in ministry, because of its effect on the interpretation of biblical teachings about women and Church leadership. The early Church had a tradition of women in leadership based on the Scriptures, but over time the interpretations and traditions changed, resulting in the exclusion of women from Church leadership roles.

No matter what tradition teaches, as Christians we are responsible to learn and understand what God's Word teaches about women in ministry. To do this effectively, we'll examine some of the traditions related to women in ministry from a biblical perspective.

Comparing traditions and the Bible can be difficult, particularly in cultures where the Bible has been influential. In such cultures, the origins of a tradition may not be clear: in some cases, a tradition exists because people found precedent for it in the Bible; other times people have taken their pre-existing traditions and justified them using the Bible. Our first step is to unravel tradition from the Bible so that we can better understand it.

The most important thing to understand in indentifying traditions is that they originate with humanity and not with God. God commands; human beings pass down traditions. The practical difficulty in separating the two arises because humanity seeks to elevate itself by cloaking its traditions in the Word of God.

We know that God is greater than humanity (Job 33:12; Isa. 55:9). But since creation, humanity has continually looked for ways to be equal with God. In Genesis, the man and the woman yielded to a temptation to be "like God," and disobeyed God, eating the fruit of the tree of the knowledge of good and evil (Gen. 3:4–6).

Later, as humanity increased in number and populated the earth, this same desire for greatness stirred all the people of the earth to build a tower that reached up to heaven—the tower of Babel:

Genesis 11:1–4

1 Now the whole earth had one language and the same words.

2 And as people migrated from the east, they found a plain in the land of Shinar and settled there.

3 And they said to one another, "Come, let us make bricks, and burn them thoroughly." And they had brick for stone, and bitumen for mortar.

4 Then they said, "Come, let us build ourselves a city and a tower with its top in the heavens, and let us make a name for ourselves, lest we be dispersed over the face of the whole earth."

These ancient people, in their desire to "make a name" for themselves, sought to reach up to heaven, which is God's domain (Isa. 66:1; Matt. 5:34–35). They wanted to reach God's domain to elevate *their* names, not His name.

But despite the plans of the builders, the story ends with them not getting anything they wanted. They didn't make a name for themselves and they were scattered across the earth—exactly the opposite of their goal (Gen. 11:7–9). This story stands as a solemn reminder to humanity that we will never be able to approach the habitation or level of God by our own efforts (Isa. 40:25; 46:5).

We should not think that this striving behavior was limited to ancient times; it is still taking place in the Church today, in a different form. Instead of trying to reach God physically, many Christians are trying to reach God's level spiritually. They do this by elevating their notions of right and wrong—their traditions—to the same level of importance as God's Word. Some believers take the idea of tradition even further, believing that God respects human traditions and expects people to uphold them.

God's Commands Are Supreme

Jesus dealt with these sorts of perspectives in Matthew 15. The scribes and Pharisees from Jerusalem dared to question Him about the hand-washing practices of His disciples. They got an earful in return:

Matthew 15:1–9

1 Then Pharisees and scribes came to Jesus from Jerusalem and said,

2 "Why do your disciples break the tradition of the elders? For they do not wash their hands when they eat."

3 He answered them, "And why do you break the commandment of God for the sake of your tradition?

> 4 For God commanded, 'Honor your father and your mother,' and, 'Whoever reviles father or mother must surely die.'
>
> 5 But you say, 'If anyone tells his father or his mother, "What you would have gained from me is given to God,"
>
> 6 he need not honor his father.' So for the sake of your tradition you have made void the word of God.
>
> 7 You hypocrites! Well did Isaiah prophesy of you, when he said:
>
> 8 "'This people honors me with their lips, but their heart is far from me;
>
> 9 in vain do they worship me, teaching as doctrines the commandments of men.'"

The first thing to notice is how the religious leaders classified the behavior of the Lord's disciples: as a transgression. The Greek word used here refers to the act of turning away from something, or of moving past something without paying attention to it. In other words, the essence of transgression is to neglect some obligation. This is why the scribes and Pharisees were upset: because Jesus' disciples weren't paying any attention to their traditions!

Jesus' response went right to the heart of the matter. He reminded the religious leaders of what transgression really is—neglect of God's Law, not their traditions (Matt. 15:6). Then Jesus pointed out that those same religious traditions they prized so highly were causing people to neglect, to *transgress* God's commands.

This narrative illustrates that human rules and traditions can be a hindrance to God's Word, because they compete with the Word for our obedience. "We must," as the Apostle Peter said, "obey God rather than men." (Acts 5:29).

These were the religious leaders that Christ was speaking to, so it was no light thing for them to be questioned about their faithfulness to God. But the situation revealed the condition of their hearts: they paid diligent attention to *their* traditions, while contradicting a clear command from God. This showed that their hearts were not really with God, but mostly with themselves (Matt. 15:8).

Notice the focus of the religious leaders. It seems ridiculous that scribes and Pharisees from Jerusalem (Matt. 15:1), the epicenter of Jewish life, were focused on hand washing before eating. *That* was the most important issue that they had to discuss with Christ! The scribes and Pharisees had access to the writings of Moses and the Prophets. Hand washing does not occupy a particular place of prominence in those writings.

Why were they paying so much attention to it? Because they were more loyal to their own teachings than to God's commands, and elevated their traditions above God's Word. As Christ taught elsewhere, a person cannot serve two masters; they are loyal to either one or to the other (Matt. 6:24; Luke 6:13). Their loyalties were with themselves.

This brings us to the second issue: the impact of human traditions upon followers of God's Word.

Human Traditions Turn From the Truth

In Titus, the Apostle Paul addressed a situation where believers had turned their attention to myths, and to human rules originating with those who had left the truth (Titus 1:10–14). This was a common refrain in Paul's letters; he often cautioned believers to avoid things which prevented them from listening to the truth:

> **2 Timothy 4:3–4**
>
> **3 For the time is coming when people will not endure sound teaching, but having itching ears they will accumulate for themselves teachers to suit their own passions,**
>
> **4 and will turn away from listening to the truth and wander off into myths.**

Here, Paul specifically warned Timothy about the things that cause people to turn from the truth: 1) an unwillingness to hear sound teaching, and 2) teachers who focus on human passions—things that people want to hear. Underneath this teaching, Paul is highlighting the opposite nature of human passions and the truth. He gave a similar warning to the Colossians:

> **Colossians 2:8**
>
> **See to it that no one takes you captive by philosophy and empty deceit, according to human tradition, according to the elemental spirits of the world, and not according to Christ.**

Notice the groupings: philosophy, deceit, human traditions and the basic principles of the world are together in one group. Opposite them, alone, is Christ.

Paul isn't the only apostle who drew attention to this distinction. The Apostle John did also:

> **1 John 2:15–16**
>
> **15 Do not love the world or the things in the world. If anyone loves the world, the love of the Father is not in him.**
>
> **16 For all that *is* in the world—the lust of the flesh, the lust of the eyes, and the pride of life—is not of the Father but is of the world.**

John presents it as an issue of love. Loving the world (including the things in it) is contrary to loving God—because the world is rooted in lust and pride, attributes which are totally inconsistent with the nature of God (Num. 23:19; Job 36:5; Phil. 2:8; 1 Pe. 5:5). Just as Christ taught that no person can serve two masters, John pointed out that the human heart cannot love God and at the same time love things that are contrary to God.

The Apostle James also agreed, noting that friendship, or even the willingness to be friendly with the things of the world makes a person God's enemy (Jas. 4:4). These verses remind us that our allegiance is singular: either to God or to human, worldly things, not to both.

The most prominent illustration of the difference between God and the world is found in Jesus Christ, who was in the world, but was not of it—He was separate from its sinfulness. Note Jesus' words before His crucifixion:

> **John 14:30, NASB**
>
> **I will not speak much more with you, for the ruler of the world is coming, and he has nothing in Me;**

He told His disciples that He had nothing in common with the ruler of this world, referring to Satan (2 Cor. 4:4). Jesus, who is the Son of God, and the ruler of this world (Satan) are opposed (Matt. 8:29; 12:24-28), so it follows naturally that the things of this world are contrary to the things of God.

Other verses confirm this opposition. In the Gospel of Matthew, Jesus observes that Satan has an interest in human or man–made things (Matt. 16:23). And Judas went out to betray the Lord *after* Satan entered him (Luke 22:3).

Finally, Jesus underscored His separateness from the world, in His prayer for His disciples:

> **John 17:14**
>
> **I have given them your word, and the world has hated them because they are not of the world, just as I am not of the world.**

In this prayer, Jesus crystallizes the opposition between the world and God: there is hatred between those who are of the world and those who are of God. With this level of opposition, it's not surprising that things coming from the world are unacceptable to God, and things from God are rejected by the world.

So what does this all mean in the discussion of human traditions and the Word of God? It means that God's Word is more important than human tradition because it comes from God, and the things of God are greater than the things of humanity. In the Church, it means that human rules and regulations that attempt to govern religious matters are highly offensive to God—why should God's matters be regulated by those who naturally oppose Him? Human traditions can never direct people to the righteousness of God (Rom. 10:3). Or, as one of Job's friends said:

> **Job 4:17, NKJV**
> **'Can a mortal be more righteous than God? Can a man be more pure than his Maker?**

Having established that God's righteousness is greater than humanity's, we turn to the question of what to do with tradition in the Church as it relates to women in ministry.

Tradition and Women in Ministry

Much of the treatment of women in ministry in today's Church is the result of human tradition, usually cloaked in biblical verses.

One of the primary arguments against women in ministry, as discussed earlier, is the fact that Christ, the apostles, and the Old Testament priests were all male. Underlying this argument is the idea that God has established a pattern (tradition) and that this pattern is God's preferred method of leadership. In other words, the argument suggests that God is traditional!

Human Traditions vs. God's Commands

But the Bible teaches precisely the opposite, where God is seen rejecting human traditions frequently—sometimes with humor! Before the twins Esau and Jacob were born, God told Rebekah that the older would serve the younger (Gen. 25:23). This was unusual, since under the law of primogeniture, the older son was traditionally the family's primary heir.

When the time came for Jacob to marry, he perhaps thought that he understood God's willingness to operate outside of social norms. So he worked for Laban seven years to marry his beautiful younger daughter Rachel, even though Rachel had an unattractive older sister who was expected to marry first. Jacob wasn't worried. God had already favored him (the younger brother) over his older brother. He knew that God wasn't limited by human traditions!

But Laban (and God) had other ideas. Jacob found himself married first to Leah and afterwards to Rachel.[1] Was God honoring tradition or rejecting it? In one sense, yes, because culturally, the older sister was to be married first. On the other hand, age was not the only thing regarded in that culture—beauty was also important. God did not allow the more beautiful sister to marry first. Think about it: if Rachel had married first, Leah may never have married at all. Was this God's way of showing compassion towards Leah?

Even after they both married Jacob, God did not allow Rachel to have all the advantages in the marriage. Leah was married before her sister and conceived a child first, as well—things of significance in their culture. More importantly, Leah was an ancestor of Jesus Christ, because she was the mother of Judah (Gen. 29:35). Rachel was more beautiful and elevated by society's standards, but she died in childbirth and was not an ancestor of the Messiah.

God allowed the older sister to marry first, but was also unwilling to allow society's traditional view of beauty to determine the ultimate end of these women. So God uses and rejects human traditions to suit His will. What this tells us is God often does things we don't expect:

Isaiah 43:19
Behold, I am doing a new thing; now it springs forth, do you not perceive it? I will make a way in the wilderness and rivers in the desert.

The idea of God doing new things is found throughout the Bible (Is. 42:9; 48:6; Jer. 31:22). When we are born again, we receive new life (Rom. 6:4), partake of the new covenant (Heb. 9:15), await a resurrection where we will receive new bodies (Rom. 8:23; 1 John 3:2), and we look forward to a new heavens and a new earth (Is. 65:17)! But despite all of this newness in Christ, we somehow forget that God does things that are new to us now, in this present time.

It is true that God is unchanging in his attributes (Mal. 3:6) and that God doesn't change His mind as humans do (Num. 23:19; 1 Sam. 15:29). But these characteristics do not prevent God from doing things that are different from our traditions—especially in His own kingdom. God's thoughts and ways are different and higher than ours (Isa. 55:9).

God also provides us with early indications of things He plans to do. When Abraham was called by God and believed God, he was uncircumcised, which indicated God's intention to reach out to uncircumcised believers. Later, Abraham was circumcised, which foreshadowed God's plan to reach circumcised believers (Rom. 4:9–12). Later, when God's actions toward the uncircumcised Gentiles appeared new to the early Church, they were mistaken—God had already developed His plan far in advance. It was the Church that had to make the adjustment and look back on the Word to understand what God had done.

Human Traditions vs. God's Commands

So we cannot look at what (we think) God has done historically and assume that God will never do things differently. God is not only able and willing to do new things in ministry, but has already done them—like when He changed the priesthood from the house of Aaron to the order of Melchizedek (Ps. 110:4, Heb. 5:10; 7:11–28).

Does this mean there is no place for tradition in the Church? No. Many human traditions in the Church are useful in fulfilling the Church's mission. Having an order of service each week allows regular attendees and visitors to follow along with what is happening during worship. Imagine how challenging it would be to attend worship services if the order of service was changed every week. This is just one example of the kind of tradition that is useful for churches.

But such traditions become problematic when they function as a yardstick of righteousness against other congregations ("that church's order of worship is not as good as ours") or in judgment ("that church's order of worship is not of God"). There is, of course, always room for traditions that are based on obedience to the Word of God and love toward others (2 Thess. 3:6).

Human culture exists, and where it does not conflict with the Word of God, Christians are to follow its customs peacefully, and not engage in shocking or troublesome behavior (Rom. 12:8; 13:7). In instances where human culture contradicts the Word of God, Christians are not required to agree with or to act in conformity with human culture (Acts 5:29). Our primary obligation is to obey the Word of God (John 14:15; Jas. 1:22).

The goal of women in ministry is not to be contrarian, nor to seek out opportunities to engage or oppose the cultures in which we live. Instead, our goal is to focus our attention on being obedient to God by accepting and fulfilling His call to ministry—even if it means rejecting traditions that don't line up with God's Word.

NOTES

1. Not surprisingly, Jacob still didn't accept cultural norms regarding birth order, even after his experience with Leah and Rachel. Towards the end of his life, when blessing Joseph's children, Jacob blessed Joseph's younger son Ephraim above the older son, Manasseh (Gen. 48:13-19). Even more surprising is that Joseph objected—Joseph who knew from experience that God often chooses the younger to bear rule.

Also, notice the parallels between Isaac's blindness when blessing Jacob over Esau and Jacob's blindness while blessing Ephraim over Manasseh. Perhaps God signified by this that His blessings are done similarly—without regard to "eyesight."

CHAPTER SEVEN
Servants or Rulers?

"Then [Jesus] came to Capernaum. And when He was in the house He asked [the disciples], "What was it you disputed among yourselves on the road?"

But they kept silent, for on the road they had disputed among themselves who would be the greatest.

And He sat down, called the twelve, and said to them, "If anyone desires to be first, he shall be last of all and servant of all."

MARK 9:33–35

Christ's teachings about greatness are a complete reversal of human notions of importance. Instead of the greatest person being the ruler, Christ taught His disciples that the greatest person was the one who served. He taught them to take the lowest place and to seek to serve others instead of ruling over them (Luke 22:24–27). Christ's own life was characterized by humility and service, even to the point of death (Phil. 2:8).

After being exposed to His teaching for years, the disciples understood how Christ viewed greatness. This is how they knew that He would disapprove of their argument about being the greatest. But today, almost 2,000 years later, many Christians have chosen to continue the disciples' argument. They remain focused on who is to be "in charge" in the Church, except now the argument focuses on men and women.

Underlying many of the arguments against women in ministry is the notion that God doesn't want women to have authority in the Church. This view is influenced, at least in part, by the idea that ministry is primarily a position of power—not a lowly position of service, as Christ taught. It's a misunderstanding of God's view of greatness.

Around the time of His crucifixion, Christ found an occasion to teach His disciples about God's perspective on greatness. They had just finished celebrating the Passover when He declared the new covenant to them, giving them bread and wine to eat and drink (Luke 22:17–20). Afterward, in a solemn moment, Christ declared His betrayer to be present with them, and seated at the table (Luke 22:21–23).

The disciples were understandably saddened for Christ and concerned about the identity of the betrayer. But their concern was short–lived because they quickly began to argue about which one of them would be the greatest (Luke 22:24). You know, which one of them would be the new leader after Christ's departure!

Jesus took that opportunity to explain God's view of greatness and how He had modeled it for them:

Luke 22:24–27

24 A dispute also arose among them, as to which of them was to be regarded as the greatest.

25 And he said to them, "The kings of the Gentiles exercise lordship over them, and those in authority over them are called benefactors.

26 But not so with you. Rather, let the greatest among you become as the youngest, and the leader as one who serves.

27 For who is the greater, one who reclines at table or one who serves? Is it not the one who reclines at table? But I am among you as the one who serves.

Jesus drew a direct contrast between those considered great in this world and those who are great in God's sight. He appealed to what the disciples already knew from their own experiences: the world considers those who rule to be the greatest. But here, and in other teachings, Jesus explicitly rejected this idea and reversed it—so that the person who is viewed as the least is actually the greatest, and the one who appears to be great is really the lesser (Matt. 20:16).

This teaching occurs in such close proximity to Christ's betrayal and crucifixion that we cannot miss the connection between His service and His death. Christ, who was humble unto death is now, though invisible to us, Lord of all. In Christ, God's view of greatness becomes plain to His disciples—it is servanthood. Those who serve in this life will one day be rewarded with authority (Matt. 25:21, Luke 19:17).

Authority or Service?

If we understand ministry as servanthood and not as ruling, it is difficult to argue that women shouldn't serve in ministry. Let's face it: no one minds women serving in church— women are Sunday school teachers, ushers, secretaries, and perform a variety of service functions. Those against women in ministry (whether men or women) don't mind one bit when women serve, as long as it's in an area that they view as "service-oriented."

But when it comes to serving as a pastor, elder, teacher, bishop or a similar role, these same Christians see those functions as authoritative and not as service—so they believe women are disqualified. But in the Bible, those who Christ chose to lead His people identified themselves as *servants* (Rom. 1:1; Jas. 1:1; 2 Pet. 1:1; Jude 1), and not as rulers. There is still a disconnect among many Christians as to what ministry actually means. It means service.

In a sense, those of us called into ministry are both servants and leaders. On one hand, we are servants of God and of the Church, but because of our role as servants of God, people will follow our behavior and conduct, thereby making us leaders. So ministry is both serving and leading. But the authority or leadership part of service is not to be sought after, nor is it the dominant characteristic of Christian ministry—it is an outgrowth of service to God. The arguments about who should have authority are just as silly now as when the disciples had them around 2,000 years ago. Our goal as Christians (including ministers) is to humble ourselves in the service of God and if and when others follow our behavior, we are to impart to them what God has given to us.

Those of us that have ministry gifts are to use them in the Church for its edification (Eph. 4:8–16) and have no authority whatsoever to act as lords over God's heritage (1 Pe. 5:3). What authority means from a spiritual perspective is that those who have responsibility will receive a heavier judgment from God (Luke 12:48; Jas. 3:1), and dare not be found inattentive to their duties (Matt. 24:48–51; Luke 12:45–46). Authority is not to be thrown around at others in order to force them to submit to your will.

Gifts From God

Christians often forget that ministries are also a service to the Church, to help it reach maturity. When Christ distributes ministry gifts to individuals, they are not as much for the individual person as much as for the benefit of the entire Church. And Christ distributes ministry gifts without regard to gender:

> **Ephesians 4:8–13**
>
> **8 Therefore it says, "When he ascended on high he led a host of captives, and he gave gifts to men."**
>
> **9 (In saying, "He ascended," what does it mean but that he had also descended into the lower regions, the earth?**
>
> **10 He who descended is the one who also ascended far above all the heavens, that he might fill all things.)**
>
> **11 And he gave the apostles, the prophets, the evangelists, the shepherds and teachers,**

> 12 to equip the saints for the work of ministry, for building up the body of Christ,
>
> 13 until we all attain to the unity of the faith and of the knowledge of the Son of God, to mature manhood, to the measure of the stature of the fullness of Christ,

The Greek word translated "men" in verse 8 is *anthropos*, meaning human (as in anthropology, the study of humankind), and includes both men and women in its use throughout the Bible. If God had intended that only males should hold these ministry gifts, a Greek word that specifically refers to males would have been used. This text plainly indicates that Christ gives the gifts of apostle, prophet, evangelist, pastor, and teacher to men *and* to women for the benefit of the Church.

This distribution of gifts also fits with the notion of God as impartial. In chapter one, we observed that God doesn't make decisions based on external appearances, such as looks, gender, wealth, or charm, the way people do (1 Sam. 16:7).

Loving the Highest Places

Another area where human importance hinders women serving in ministry is the desire of current leaders to maintain and secure their "high" positions. The Scripture includes plenty of examples of these types of people; in Christ's day, often the religious leaders: Pharisees, Sadducees, scribes, and lawyers.

These leaders had the greatest intellectual knowledge of the Word of God during Christ's time on earth, but did not recognize that the Word had become flesh and walked among them (John 1:1–4, 14). Not only this, but they also rejected and helped to crucify Him, fulfilling the very Scriptures they claimed to understand.

Of course they didn't see it this way. They believed that they were serving God, but had unwittingly become His enemies, and were fighting against Him. Such behaviors are commonly shown by those who love their positions more than God.

So it is not surprising that the Lord reserved His harshest words for these types of leaders. He was especially disgusted with their hypocrisy (Matt. 23:13–15; Luke 11:44) and their self-importance:

> **Luke 11:43**
>
> **Woe to you Pharisees! For you love the best seat in the synagogues and greetings in the marketplaces.**

Jesus' condemnation wasn't just about the actions of the religious leaders, it was also about the eventual results of their conduct:

> **Luke 20:45–47**
>
> **45 Then, in the hearing of all the people, He said to His disciples,**
>
> **46 "Beware of the scribes, who desire to go around in long robes, love greetings in the marketplaces, the best seats in the synagogues, and the best places at feasts,**
>
> **47 "who devour widows' houses, and for a pretense make long prayers. These will receive greater condemnation."**

It is evident from these passages that the Lord did not approve of the leaders' showiness, or their efforts at self-promotion. In John's Gospel, we get a look at some behind-the-scenes action involving the chief priests and Pharisees, while they talked about the Lord:

> **John 11:47–48**
>
> **47 So the chief priests and the Pharisees gathered the Council and said, "What are we to do? For this man performs many signs.**

Servants or Rulers?

> **48** If we let him go on like this, everyone will believe in him, and the Romans will come and take away both our place and our nation."

Among themselves, they acknowledge that the Lord has done many signs, but they didn't consider the meaning of the signs. Had they thought about it, they would have realized that, at a minimum, Christ was a prophet of God. They had access to the Jewish Scriptures, which have numerous examples of God's prophets performing miracles that were very similar to those performed by the Lord, such as healings (2 Kgs. 5:8–14), raising the dead (1 Kgs. 17:17–24), and the multiplication of food (2 Kgs. 4:42–44).

But these religious leaders were indifferent to the Lord's miracles and what they signified. Instead, they were mostly worried about losing their position and their nation. They were not only concerned more about themselves than with God, but, despite their pretenses, they were more concerned about their position than their own nation!

Plenty of Christian leaders carry this mindset today. They are primarily concerned about maintaining their "positions" in the Church, and are against women in ministry partially because the women might take their roles. Not surprisingly, their focus on power results in their blindness to what the Scriptures teach about women in ministry. So they continue misusing the Bible against women in their quest to retain power.

Why are they blind? For the same reason that the religious leaders were blind to Jesus' ministry during His life. Sin, especially an unwillingness to hear, always blinds people to the truth of God (Isa. 6:8-10; Matt. 13:10–15). For many Christian leaders today, it is more important to retain power than for God's will to be done concerning women in ministry.

When Power Corrupts

Some Christian leaders become so consumed by their desire to hold onto power that they begin to oppress those in their congregations, and also end up working against God. The New Testament provides an example of such a person. In the Book of Third John, the apostle mentions a man named Diotrephes, and noted the lengths he went to in order to control his position in the local congregation:

> **3 John 1:9–11, NASB**
>
> **9** I wrote something to the church; but Diotrephes, who loves to be first among them, does not accept what we say.
>
> **10** For this reason, if I come, I will call attention to his deeds which he does, unjustly accusing us with wicked words; and not satisfied with this, he himself does not receive the brethren, either, and he forbids those who desire to do so and puts them out of the church.
>
> **11** Beloved, do not imitate what is evil, but what is good. The one who does good is of God; the one who does evil has not seen God.

Diotrephes is described as a person who loved to have the preeminence in the church. His desire for power led to some very questionable conduct on his part. First, he spoke against the Apostle John and his John's fellow workers. Then he refused to receive other Christian brethren, including some of the other apostles. Next he forbade anyone to help the Apostle John and his fellow workers. Finally, he went to those who wanted to help John and his colleagues and threw them out of the congregation.

We aren't given much information on the story surrounding Diotrephes, but here's what we can gather: he professed to be converted to Christ, or else he wouldn't have been a member of the congregation. He had provided sufficient evidence of Christian conduct that he was elevated to a position of leadership in the local church. He also had some authority, because he was able to threaten church members and had power to throw people out of the congregation.

But he used his power to entrench himself at the top. And it gets worse.

The sinfulness of Diotrephes' conduct is aggravated because of the times in which he lived. In the early days of the Church, the information held by direct eyewitnesses of Christ was extremely valuable. During the time that 1, 2, and 3 John were written, the early Church did not yet have a complete canon of New Testament writings, like what we have today. They probably had access to some of the Old Testament (Jewish) scriptures, and some of the apostle's other writings.

But information did not spread back then with the ease of today's technology, and there were letters being sent around that falsely claimed to be from the apostles (2 Thess. 2:1). So one of Christ's apostles or anyone who actually knew Christ in the flesh was able to speak with great authority on the doctrine and teachings of Christ. This was very important to the edification and survival of the local congregations.

But Diotrephes didn't care about this. He was unconcerned that the congregation would benefit from hearing those who walked with Christ. Instead he refused the apostles and kicked out anyone who would receive them. By his actions, he became the enemy of the very God who he was claiming to serve—just like the religious leaders of Christ's day.

Are you really surprised that those opposing women in ministry today are most often the religious leaders—as were the scribes and Pharisees? These are the same people who claim the greatest command of the Bible, or are in leadership in local churches who simply want to retain their high positions. Such leaders insist that they are followers of the true God, and will cite Scripture to prove it, but in works they deny God (Titus 1:16) by hindering the work of God's female servants.

What it Means to Be a Servant

As Christians, we must remember that God is the one to be served. *Only* God is great, and the rest of us are God's children, servants and friends—or else we are His enemies. Jesus addressed the issue of service to God in one of His many parables:

> **Luke 17:7–10**
>
> **7 "Will any one of you who has a servant plowing or keeping sheep say to him when he has come in from the field, 'Come at once and recline at table'?**
>
> **8 Will he not rather say to him, 'Prepare supper for me, and dress properly, and serve me while I eat and drink, and afterward you will eat and drink'?**
>
> **9 Does he thank the servant because he did what was commanded?**
>
> **10 So you also, when you have done all that you were commanded, say, 'We are unworthy servants; we have only done what was our duty.'"**

As servants, our obedience to God does not merit thanks—rather, when we have done what we are commanded, we must remember that we have only done our duty. For those of us in ministry, it's a reminder that ministry is primarily service to God; the lordship itself belongs to God.

There is also a reward to be found in service. In the Gospel of Luke, the Lord was preparing to eat bread on the Sabbath at the house of one of the chief Pharisees. While there, the Lord observed that everyone was choosing the best places to sit, which provided another perfect opportunity for a lesson:

Servants or Rulers?

> **Luke 14:7–11**
>
> 7 Now he told a parable to those who were invited, when he noticed how they chose the places of honor, saying to them,
>
> 8 "When you are invited by someone to a wedding feast, do not sit down in a place of honor, lest someone more distinguished than you be invited by him,
>
> 9 and he who invited you both will come and say to you, 'Give your place to this person,' and then you will begin with shame to take the lowest place.
>
> 10 But when you are invited, go and sit in the lowest place, so that when your host comes he may say to you, 'Friend, move up higher.' Then you will be honored in the presence of all who sit at table with you.
>
> 11 For everyone who exalts himself will be humbled, and he who humbles himself will be exalted."

With God, those who honor themselves will find that God sees others as more honorable than them, and they will be humbled. Those who humbly take the lowest place will find that God sees them as more honorable than they realized, they will receive exaltation from Him.

If you are a woman called by the Lord into His service, take courage from His words and continue doing just as you have been commanded: serve.

A reward and honor from God awaits you.

EPILOGUE
Preparing for The Lord's Return

"Behold, He is coming with clouds..."

REVELATION 1:7

If you just finished reading this book and realize that you haven't accepted God's calling on your life—the time to get serious about God's will for your life is now. The Word of God teaches us that "[n]ow is the accepted time...now is the day of salvation (2 Cor. 6:2). God also warns us against procrastinaton: "[t]oday if you will hear His voice, harden not your hearts..." (Heb. 3:7–8).

To get serious, spend time with the Lord daily in prayer and study of the Word. Ask Him for guidance concerning His will for your life (Prov. 3:5–6; 2 Tim. 2:15; Jas. 1:5–6).

Even if you are not called to full-time ministry, it is still important to find out God's will for your life, because God calls each one of His people to serve (Luke 22:26–27; Gal. 5:13). There is work for you to do!

If you realize that you (may) have been hindering women whom God has called—whether you are male or female—take the necessary steps to support women who you believe are called by God, through prayer and encouraging words (Matt. 3:8; 2 Cor. 7:11).

For those of you called by God, remember to take advantage of every opportunity to obey God, while you are able to do so (Heb. 2:1). Do not delay the start of your obedience to God. You should not feel the need to be in a hurry (Prov. 19:2), but it is wise to begin praying and seek the Lord about His will for your life. The Lord reminded His followers that when He returns, He will require them to account for their actions and activities:

> **Matthew 24:45–51**
>
> 45 "Who then is the faithful and wise servant, whom his master has set over his household, to give them their food at the proper time?
>
> 46 Blessed is that servant whom his master will find so doing when he comes.
>
> 47 Truly, I say to you, he will set him over all his possessions.
>
> 48 But if that wicked servant says to himself, 'My master is delayed,'
>
> 49 and begins to beat his fellow servants and eats and drinks with drunkards,
>
> 50 the master of that servant will come on a day when he does not expect him and at an hour he does not know
>
> 51 and will cut him in pieces and put him with the hypocrites. In that place there will be weeping and gnashing of teeth.

These are the words of the Lord. And though they seem harsh, we must take them as they are written. It is a serious sin against God to ignore the gifts He has given to you, or to fail to use those gifts for the edification of the Body of Christ. According to the Lord, any of His servants who fail to perform the responsibilities assigned to her, who begins living in a careless and unloving way, and who begins to indulge the flesh, will have the same end as the hypocrites—an eternity apart from God.

It is time to get busy fulfilling the will of God for your life—and as you do so, may God go with you.

Author's Note

"...of making many books there is no end, and much study is a weariness to the flesh."

ECCLESIASTES 12:12

When I began writing this book in 2006, I had no idea that it would take me so long to finish! I had written quite a bit of it, and outlined the rest, and then seminary, another book project, and life got in the way of finishing. It is indeed sweet to put the finishing touches on this manuscript.

This book is the culmination of a considerable amount of study and prayer, and would not have been possible without the love, support, and prayers of my friends, family, and ministry mentors.

In particular, I'd like to thank my mother, Lena Smith Carter, for her gracious support and kindness, and for her help with this project. I am also grateful to my friends who were kind enough to read and critique the most recent draft(s) of the manuscript: Jordan May, Ivy Bennett, and Heather Evans. Thanks also to Brother Zollie Smith, who always has a kind, encouraging, and scriptural Word, as well as to my Facebook supporters—it's great have so many fans of the book already!

I am really grateful to Angi Shearstone, the designer of the beautiful cover art, for her patience and professionalism. The final version was beyond what I hoped.

Above all, I would like to thank the Holy Spirit for the idea of this book, which He placed in my heart so many years ago. May His Word be a blessing to all who hear and read it.

APPENDIX A
Believe on the Lord Jesus Christ

God Loves You
For God so loved the world, that he gave his only Son, that whoever believes in him should not perish but have eternal life. (John 3:16)

But God shows his love for us in that while we were still sinners, Christ died for us. (Rom. 5:8)

But Your Sins Keep You and God Apart
Behold, the LORD's hand is not shortened, that it cannot save, or his ear dull, that it cannot hear; but your iniquities have made a separation between you and your God, and your sins have hidden his face from you so that he does not hear. (Isa. 59:1-2)

God Sent Jesus to Bring You Closer To God
By taking on the penalty of your sins, which is death.
For I delivered to you as of first importance what I also received: that Christ died for our sins in accordance with the Scriptures (1 Cor. 15:3)

But Jesus rose from the dead, and we are reconciled to God through Him.
For if while we were enemies we were reconciled to God by the death of his Son, much more, now that we are reconciled, shall we be saved by his life. More than that, we also rejoice in God through our Lord Jesus Christ, through whom we have now received reconciliation. (Rom. 5:10-11)

Believe on the Lord Jesus Christ
Believe in the Lord Jesus, and you will be saved (Acts 16:31).

...if you confess with your mouth that Jesus is Lord and believe in your heart that God raised him from the dead, you will be saved. For with the heart one believes and is justified, and with the mouth one confesses and is saved. (Rom. 10:9-10)

If you believe that Jesus Christ died for your sins and that God raised him from the dead, below is a prayer for you to confess (acknowledge) your faith in Jesus Christ:

> **God, I believe that your Son, Jesus Christ, died on the cross for my sins. I believe that You raised Him from the dead so that I could be reconciled to You. I ask for your guidance and wisdom, so that I might live my life in a way that is pleasing to you. Thank you for the gift of your Son and for your many blessings. In Jesus' name, Amen.**

If you have prayed this prayer, please email us at info@troublingher.com. We will pray for you and get you some materials that will help you learn more about your walk with God.

APPENDIX B
Reading and Discussion Questions

---

1. Describe some of the common errors of interpretation that impact the discussion of women in ministry? What are some ways to avoid these errors?

2. Name two biblical narratives that are often interpreted with bias against women (in ministry). What are some more balanced ways to understand those narratives?

3. What does Jesus' incarnation, ministry, death, and resurrection teach us about God's willingness to accomplish His purposes through women?

4. Did you learn something new about some of the women in the Bible? If so, which ones? What did her story teach you about women in ministry?

5. Why do we need to be careful when studying Bible verses about women and wives? What are some of the difficulties in understanding such verses?

6. In creation, God gave woman dominion over the earth along with man. How does this make you feel? Does it change the limitations you put on yourself?

7. What are some of the things that make the Apostle Paul's writings so difficult to understand?

8. What are some biblical ways to respond when someone says that they don't believe women should be ministers or elders, or have authority in the Church?

Index

GENESIS
Gen. 1-3 60
Gen. 1:26–27 6
Gen. 1:26–28 33,38
Gen. 2:7 35
Gen. 2:18 35
Gen. 2:15–18 64
Gen. 2:18–23 6
Gen. 2:21-22 65
Gen. 3:1 37
Gen. 3:1–4 67
Gen. 3:4–6 72
Gen. 3:6 37
Gen. 3:9–13 38
Gen. 3:12 38
Gen. 3:16 38
Gen. 3:14 35
Gen. 3:15 37,52,68,69
Gen. 3:16 37,38
Gen. 3:17 37
Gen. 3:17–19 38
Gen. 3:19 37
Gen. 4:1–2 61
Gen. 4:7 42
Gen. 4:8 63
Gen. 5:2 34
Gen. 5:3 34
Gen. 5:15 18,44
Gen. 9:6 35,37
Gen. 11:1–4 72
Gen. 11:7–9 73
Gen. 12:1-3 56
Gen. 14:17-20 56
Gen. 14:19 56
Gen. 14:20 56
Gen. 17:10–27 46
Gen. 17:15–21 61
Gen. 18:12 32
Gen. 21:12 15,61
Gen. 25:23 61,79
Gen. 25:23–26 61
Gen. 25:26 52

Gen. 27:35-36 52
Gen. 29:35 79
Gen. 37:5–11 61
Gen. 42:6 61
Gen. 43:26 61
Gen. 45:4–8 64
Gen. 48:13-19 82

EXODUS
Exod. 1:15–22 39,69
Exod. 2:4 19,69
Exod. 2:6–10 69
Exod. 12:49 30
Exod. 15:20–21 19
Exod. 18:13-16 20
Exod. 23:12 3
Exod. 28:1 18,44,56

LEVITICUS
Lev. 11:4 8
Lev. 15:25 50
Lev. 19:36 31
Lev. 20:10 28,63
Lev. 21:1 18,44
Lev. 22:30-23 8
Lev. 24:22 30

NUMBERS
Num. 3:10-13 56
Num. 5:6–7 63
Num. 12:1–9 19
Num. 12:2 19
Num. 12:6 19
Num. 12:15 32
Num. 15:14–16 46
Num. 23:19 80
Num. 26:59 19

DEUTERONOMY
Deut. 5:13–14 3
Deut. 10:17 13

Deut. 17:6 10
Deut. 19:15 9
Deut. 24:1 25,48
Deut. 25:13 31
Deut. 32:43 56

JOSHUA
Josh. 1:14 36

JUDGES
Judg. 2:11-16 19
Judg. 2:16-19 20
Judg. 4:3–4 19
Judg. 4:5 20
Judg. 4:6–10 20
Judg. 13:2–5 69
Judg. 13:9 69
Judg. 13:10–14 69

1 SAMUEL
1 Sam. 1:1–20 69
1 Sam. 15:29 80
1 Sam. 16:11 62
1 Sam. 16:6 62
1 Sam 16:7 9,31,87
1 Sam. 17:13 62
1 Sam. 17:15-17 20

1 KINGS
1 Kgs. 17:17–24 89
1 Kgs. 18:13 63

2 KINGS
2 Kgs. 4:27–35 4
2 Kgs. 4:42–44 89
2 Kgs. 5:8–14 89
2 Kgs. 5:9–15 4
2 Kgs. 22:14-16 21

2 CHRONICLES
2 Chr. 9:1–12 39

2 Chr. 19:7 13,29
2 Chr. 35:18 21

Nehemiah
Neh. 9:6 29

Job
Job 4:17 78
Job 33:12 72
Job 36:5 76

Psalms
Ps. 41:9 52
Ps. 51:5 62
Ps. 68:31 46
Ps. 110:4 56,81

Proverbs
Prov. 3:5–6 97
Prov. 11:14 1
Prov. 17:3 9
Prov. 19:2 95
Prov. 20:10 30
Prov. 20:12 xii
Prov. 20:23 30
Prov. 22:2 ....13, 29,40
Prov. 31:16 39

Ecclesiastes
Eccl. 12:12 97

Isaiah
Isa. 6:8-10 89
Isa. 11:19–25 46
Isa. 40:25 73
Isa. 42:9 80
Isa. 43:19 80
Isa. 46:5 73
Isa. 48:6 80
Isa. 50:9 36
Isa. 55:9 72,80
Isa. 59:1-2 98
Isa. 66:1 73
Isa. 65:17 80

Jeremiah
Jer. 31:22 80

Ezekiel
Ezek. 3:10 xii
Ezek. 18:29 31

Daniel
Daniel 10:13 36

Micah
Mic. 6:4 19
Mic. 6:11 31

Malachi
Mal. 3:6 80

Matthew
Matt. 1:1 18,44,47
Matt. 1:21 18,44
Matt. 3:8 95
Matt. 5:11–12 55
Matt. 5:17 25
Matt. 5:34–35 73
Matt. 6:24 75
Matt. 8:29 77
Matt. 12:24-28 77
Matt. 13:10–15 89
Matt. 15:1 75
Matt. 15:1–3 73
Matt. 15:4-9 74
Matt. 15:6 71,74
Matt. 15:8 75
Matt. 15:16-18 70
Matt. 15:21–28 46
Matt. 16:16–17 50
Matt. 16:22–23 63
Matt. 16:23 77
Matt. 17:1–3 64
Matt. 17:1–8 70
Matt. 18:15–16 10
Matt. 19:3–6 47
Matt. 19:4 33,48
Matt. 19:6 48
Matt. 20:16 85
Matt. 22:15-22 40

Matt. 23:13–15 88
Matt. 23:23–24 7
Matt. 24:45–51 96
Matt. 24:48–51 86
Matt. 25:21 85
Matt. 26:6–13 ix
Matt. 26:69–75 63
Matt. 27:55-56 47,52,53
Matt. 27:61 47,53
Matt. 28:1-7 53
Matt. 28:8-10 53

Mark
Mark 5:25–34 50
Mark 9:33–35 83
Mark 10:10–12 24
Mark 10:11–12 ....25, 63
Mark 10:12 27
Mark 14:8 51
Mark 14:9 51
Mark 15:40-41 52
Mark 15:47 53
Mark 16:1-8 53
Mark 16:9-11 53
Mark 23:55-56 56

Luke
Luke 1:26-38 43,52
Luke 1:35 43
Luke 1:39–45 43
Luke 2:7 52
Luke 3:8 44
Luke 6:13 75
Luke 7:1–10 46
Luke 8:1–2 43
Luke 8:1–3 26,47
Luke 10:38–42 49
Luke 11:13 55
Luke 11:43 89
Luke 11:44 89
Luke 12:8 41
Luke 12:45–46 86
Luke 12:48 86
Luke 13:10–17 3,50
Luke 13:15–16 6
Luke 14:7–11 93

Index

Luke 14:26 25
Luke 17:7–10 92
Luke 19:17 85
Luke 20:45–47 88
Luke 21:12–15 55
Luke 22:3 52,64,77,83
Luke 22:17–20 84
Luke 22:21–23 84
Luke 22:24 84
Luke 22:24–27 83,84
Luke 22:26–27 95
Luke 22:31–32 63
Luke 22:55–62 63
Luke 23:49 47,52
Luke 23:55–24:3 47
Luke 24:1-11 53
Luke 24:31 xii
Luke 24:39 35

JOHN

John 1:1 18,45
John 1:1–3 41
John 1:1–4 87
John 1:14 35,87
John 3:3 39
John 3:16 98
John 4:7–42 46
John 4:16–18 48
John 4:24 34
John 4:25–26 48
John 4:27 48
John 4:39 48
John 8:3-6 27
John 8:3–11 37-38
John 8:6–9 28
John 8:10–11 28
John 11:25–27 50
John 11:47 88
John 11:48 89
John 12:23-24 53
John 13:12–15 39
John 13:18 52
John 13:20 44
John 13:27 52,64
John 13:34 39
John 14:9 41
John 14:15 81
John 14:26 36
John 14:23 42
John 14:30 77
John 17:14 77
John 19:25-27 51
John 20:11-18 53

ACTS

Acts 1:8–15 47
Acts 1:9–14 54
Acts 1:12–15 26
Acts 2:1–4 26,54
Acts 2:7 18,44
Acts 2:14–18 54
Acts 2:38 55
Acts 4:18 xi
Acts 4:19–20 xi
Acts 5:1–11 63
Acts 5:29 74,81
Acts 8:3 55
Acts 8:27–28 39
Acts 10:14 45
Acts 10:44–46 45
Acts 10:45 55
Acts 11:1–3 45
Acts 16:14 xii
Acts 16:14–15 39
Acts 16:31 98
Acts 17:24 29
Acts 18:26 22
Acts 20:27 1
Acts 22:3 49,58,62

ROMANS

Rom. 1:1 85
Rom. 2:11 11,13
Rom. 4:9–10 46
Rom. 4:9–12 80
Rom. 5:8 98
Rom. 5:10-11 98
Rom. 5:12 34,37,62
Rom. 5:12–14 38
Rom. 5:18 37
Rom. 6:4 80
Rom. 6:6 39
Rom. 6:23 37
Rom. 8:23 35,80
Rom. 9:11–13 61
Rom. 10:3 78
Rom. 10:9 99
Rom. 10:10 100
Rom. 12:8 81
Rom. 13:1 20
Rom. 13:7 81
Rom. 16:1 24,39
Rom. 16:3-5 22
Rom. 16:21 24

1 CORINTHIANS

1 Cor. 6:19 39
1 Cor. 7:4 15
1 Cor. 7:5 67
1 Cor. 7:8 17,69
1 Cor. 7:12-16 17
1 Cor. 11:5 17
1 Cor. 14:34-35 16,17
1 Cor. 15:3 98

2 CORINTHIANS

2 Cor. 2:10–12 67
2 Cor. 4:4 34,41,77
2 Cor. 5:17 39
2 Cor. 5:19 41
2 Cor. 6:2 95
2 Cor. 7:11 95
2 Cor. 11:3 37
2 Cor. 11:13 38
2 Cor. 13:1 10

GALATIANS

Gal. 3:16 18,44
Gal. 5:13 95

EPHESIANS

Eph. 1:20 xii
Eph. 2:8 68
Eph. 4:8–11 86
Eph. 4:8–16 87
Eph. 4:12-13 87
Eph. 4:13 87
Eph. 5:1 13
Eph. 5:21 15

Eph. 5:21-22 14
Eph. 5:21-23 15
Eph. 5:25 15
Eph. 5:28 15
Eph. 6:1-9 15

PHILIPPIANS
Phil. 2:8 .... 80, 87

COLOSSIANS
Col. 1:15 41
Col. 2:8 76
Col. 2:12-15 53

2 THESSALONIANS
2 Thess. 2:1 91
2 Thess. 3:6 81

1 TIMOTHY
1 Tim. 2:5 34
1 Tim. 2:11–15 59
1 Tim. 2:13-15 60
1 Tim. 2:14 .... 37, 62, 67
1 Tim. 2:15 68
1 Tim. 3:1-2 26
1 Tim. 3:8-13 23
1 Tim. 3:16 .... 18, 45
1 Tim. 5: 9–16 67
1 Tim. 5:19 10

2 TIMOTHY
2 Tim. 1:14 39
2 Tim. 2:15 95
2 Tim. 4:3–4 75

TITUS
Titus 1:10–14 75
Titus 1:16 92

HEBREWS
Heb. 2:1 95
Heb. 2:4 55
Heb. 3:7–8 95
Heb. 5:10 81
Heb. 7:7 56
Heb. 7:11–28 81

Heb. 8:6 22
Heb. 9:15 80
Heb. 11:32 20

JAMES
Jas. 1:1 85
Jas. 1:5–6 95
Jas. 1:22 81
Jas. 2:1 11
Jas. 2:1-9 12
Jas. 3:1 86
Jas. 4:4 77

1 PETER
1 Pet 1:17 29
1 Pet 3:5 14
1 Pet. 3:6 15
1 Pet. 3:8 15
1 Pet. 5:3 86
1 Pet. 5:5 .... 15, 76

2 PETER
2 Pet. 1:1 85
2 Pet. 3:16 59

1 JOHN
1 John 2:15–16 76
1 John 3:2 80
1 John 3:4 28
1 John 3:8 39

3 JOHN
3 John 1:9–11 90

JUDE
Jude 1 85

REVELATION
Rev. 1:7 95

About the Author

Jessica Faye Carter is the founder of Crosswords Evangelistic Association and The Cloud, an online community for Christian women. Her writing has appeared in *Assemblies of God Heritage* magazine and *The Pneuma Review*. She is also the author of *Double Outsiders: How Women of Color Can Succeed in Corporate America* (JIST Works, 2007) an award-winning look at professional women of color/multicultural women in the workplace and in their communities. She was previously a corporate lawyer and holds an M.Div. from Princeton Theological Seminary, a J.D. and an M.B.A. from Duke University, and a B.A. from Spelman College.

Colophon

The title font is Palatino Bold Italic; the subtitle is Felix Titling. The text and heading fonts are Palatino. The cover design is by Angie Shearstone. The cover photograph is by Maria Adelaide Silva, licensed through fotolia.com.

Coming in 2011

Questions in the Word:
A Collection of Essays

By Jessica Faye Carter

Visit The Cloud
An Online Community of Christian Women

http://cloudwomen.com
http://twitter.com/cloudwomen

Notes

Notes

Notes

Notes

Notes

Notes

Lightning Source UK Ltd.
Milton Keynes UK
UKOW02f1911140515

251552UK00001B/119/P

9 780578 034546